Easy Knitted Accessories

Easy
Knitted
Accessories

FUNKY AND FASHIONABLE PROJECTS FOR THE NOVICE KNITTER

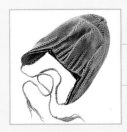

Jeanette Trotman

krause publications
An F&W Publications Company

A QUARTO BOOK

Published in North America in 2004
by Krause Publications
700 East State Street
Iola, WI 54990-0001

Library of Congress Cataloging-in-
Publication Data is available upon request

ISBN 0-87349-904-2

Conceived, designed, and produced by
Quarto Publishing plc
The Old Brewery
6 Blundell Street
London N7 9BH

QUA: EKA

Editor Michelle Pickering
Designer Elizabeth Healey
Photographer Sian Irvine
Photography assistant Leo Acker
Models Kelly Burgess, Natalie Loren,
Tracey Lushington
Make-up artist Jackie Jones
Illustrator Jennie Dooge
Pattern checker Eva Yates
Indexer Dorothy Frame
Assistant art director Penny Cobb

Art director Moira Clinch
Publisher Piers Spence

Manufactured by Star Standard
(Pte) Ltd, Singapore
Printed by Pica Digital, Singapore

contents

continued
on next page ▶

Chunky ribbed scarf **38**

Cozy cashmere hat **52**

Lacy beaded scarf **66**

Bright beaded mittens **40**

Beaded pompon scarf **54**

Chunky ruffle beanie **70**

Shaggy chenille wrap **44**

Classic-style gloves **56**

Warm winter muff **72**

Furry bag **46**

Legwarmers **59**

Funky fingerless gloves
and wrist warmers **74**

Silky socks **48**

Patchwork bag **62**

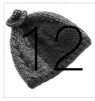
Pretty floral bag **79**

introduction

The craft of knitting is enjoying a well-deserved revival and fashion accessories such as bags, scarves, and hats have never been more popular. Whether new to the craft or a more experienced knitter, this book gives you the opportunity to combine creativity and style to make fun, funky, individual accessories.

At the beginning of the book you will find a summary of all the basic skills you will need to start making your own accessories—holding the needles, casting on, knit and purl stitches, and simple shaping techniques. From here, the real fun starts, with 30 easy-to-follow projects. The photographs show what your finished project should look like, while new skills explained within the layout of the projects allow you to learn or brush up on a relevant technique without having to flick back to the beginning of the book.

The 30 projects vary in size and the purpose of this book is to encourage you to use all types of yarn, from basic wools to cashmere blends, and sportweight to bulky weight. There is something for all levels of skill. For the new knitter, there are projects in bulky yarns that require no shaping and can be finished in a weekend. For the more experienced knitter, there are fully fashioned, lace, and intarsia projects to get to grips with. In between, allow yourself to enjoy working with an assortment of color, texture, and embellishment that will help you to produce accessories that are as enjoyable to create as they will be to use.

Some of the projects in this book use luxury yarns such as silk or cashmere—don't be discouraged. You can substitute a less expensive yarn to allow yourself to get a feel for the technique and then use expensive yarns as you become more confident. Whatever you decide to knit first, relax, take your time, and indulge in one project at a time.

Where to start

All of the projects in this book are quick and easy to make, but you will find that some are quicker and easier than others. Each knitter learns at a different pace, so what is easy for one person may not be easy for another. If you have been knitting for a few years, you should be able to tackle any of the projects. If you are completely new to knitting, start with the simpler projects and work your way up to the more complex ones as you gain confidence. Accessories are great things for the novice knitter to make because they allow you to experiment with new skills and yarns on a small, easy-to-manage scale. The 30 projects in this book can be categorized into three levels:

LEVEL 1

Easy, straightforward accessories, without much shaping or complicated stitch work, and only simple color changing. These are ideal for the novice knitter.

LEVEL 2

These are not complicated but they do have a bit more shaping, color changing, and detailed stitch work. They are suitable for the average knitter.

LEVEL 3

These accessories are a bit more challenging, involving more complex beading, shaping, and color changing. Try these once you are confident at the previous two levels.

materials,
tools
& techniques

THE FANTASTIC THING ABOUT KNITTING IS THAT YOU DON'T NEED MUCH TO

GET STARTED—JUST A PAIR OF NEEDLES AND SOME YARN. AS YOU BECOME

MORE EXPERIENCED, YOU WILL REQUIRE A RANGE OF NEEDLE SIZES AND

LENGTHS AS WELL AS OTHER KNITTING ACCESSORIES—BUY THEM AS YOU

NEED THEM. THIS CHAPTER SUMMARIZES ALL THE MATERIALS, TOOLS, AND

BASIC TECHNIQUES THAT ARE USED TO MAKE THE PROJECTS IN THIS BOOK.

Materials

The only essential material you need to make the accessories in this book is yarn. Although the specific yarns used to make the projects are listed on pages 126–127, you may wish to knit a project using a different yarn. Understanding the qualities of the various types of yarn available will help you choose one that is suitable.

Yarn

Yarn is made by spinning fibers of natural and/or synthetic material together. The combination of fibers used produces yarns of different softness and strength, which affects the look and feel of the finished item as well as what the yarn is like to knit with.

Natural fibers

Natural fibers are obtained from either animal or plant origin. Traditionally, wool has been the most popular yarn for hand knitting because of its ability to keep out the cold and wet. Advances in textile technology have made it possible to apply a shrink-resist treatment to wool yarn, making it machine washable. Untreated wool shrinks or "felts" when machine washed, and this can be used to advantage because the fabric produced is durable and can be cut without unraveling. Alpaca and angora fibers tend to be long and create a fluffy fabric with a very soft

feel when knitted. Cashmere and silk are beautifully soft but are comparatively expensive because they are regarded as luxury yarns.

Natural fibers of plant origin include cotton, linen, hemp, and ramie/jute. These do not have the same natural elasticity as wool but are ideal for warmer temperatures because they are cool to wear. Cotton is available either combed or with a mercerized coating that gives the yarn a luster that makes it particularly good for showing up stitch detail. When knitted, either type washes well and is cool to wear.

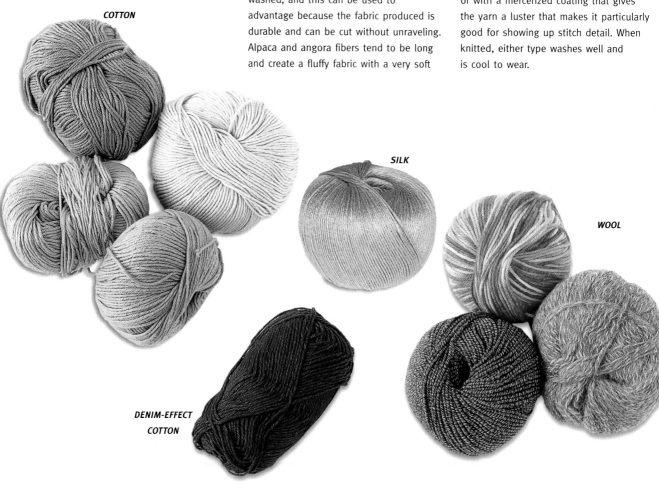

COTTON

SILK

WOOL

DENIM-EFFECT COTTON

VISCOSE/POLYESTER

Synthetic yarns

These include rayon, acrylic, polyester, lycra, and nylon. They are sometimes blended with plant fibers to make them more elastic and help them retain their shape when knitted. Synthetic yarns tend to be cheaper than those made from natural fibers because they cost less to manufacture and are often machine washable. Viscose rayon is actually manufactured from wood pulp and yarns have also been developed in recent years from recycled plastic bottles, textiles, milk, and bamboo.

Fancy yarns

Fancy yarns like chenille, lurex, and "fur" can be knitted by themselves or combined with other yarns to create exciting textural effects and contrasts. They can also be used to create interesting embroidered details after knitting. Specialty yarns are available to produce particular effects, such as denim-effect cotton, which is designed to shrink and fade like jeans.

CHENILLE AND "FUR"

Yarn weights

Each strand of fiber used to make yarn is called a ply, and different types of yarn are made from different numbers of plies. The type of fiber, number of plies, and method of spinning all affect the thickness and weight of the finished yarn. Traditionally, there were standard thicknesses of yarn, such as sport and bulky. However, as technology has developed and more fibers are blended to create a broader range of unusual yarns, these terms have become less standardized and the term bulky may be used for different weights of yarn from one yarn spinner to another.

The weights of yarn used in this book are:

Fingering Very fine yarn designed for crochet work and used in this book for embellishment.

Sport Fine yarn generally knitted on size 3 (3mm or 3.25mm) needles.

DK (double knitting) Around twice the thickness of sport and usually knitted on size 6 or 7 (4mm or 4.5mm) needles.

Aran About twice the thickness of DK, this knits up quickly on size 8 or 9 (5mm or 5.5mm) needles.

Bulky This can be anything thicker than Aran and may be knitted on size 11 to 36 (8mm to 20mm) needles.

LINEN

13

Ball bands

Whether it comes in ball or hank form, the yarn you buy will have a band around it that lists a lot of useful information.

1 Company brand and yarn name.
2 Weight and length—This tells you the weight of the yarn in ounces or grams and the yardage or meterage. This is useful when calculating how many balls you need to make a project.
3 Fiber content.
4 Shade number and dye lot—These are not the same. The manufacturer's shade number refers to a specific color. The dye lot number refers to a particular batch of yarn dyed in that color. When buying yarns for a project, try to ensure that balls of one color are all from the same dye lot. Where possible, keep ball bands or make a note of dye lots for reference.
5 Needle size—This is a generally recommended needle size. The pattern instructions for your project will tell you which specific size to use. Be aware that the needles required for each project have been chosen to create a particular feel to the finished fabric and may seem very different from those stated on the ball band.
6 Recommended gauge—This tells you the standard gauge for the yarn using the recommended needle size, usually given as a number of stitches and rows measured over 4in (10cm) of stockinette stitch.
7 Washing instructions—These tell you how you should wash and care for the yarn once knitted.

TIP: SUBSTITUTE YARNS

As a general guide, if you cannot find the specific yarn used in a project, look at the recommended needle size and gauge provided on the ball band of the yarn that was used in this book (see pages 126–127). Choose a substitute yarn that matches these as closely as possible, but be aware that the quantity of yarn required may be different.

Beads

Working with beads adds a touch of glamour to your knitting. When choosing beads, check whether or not they are machine washable. Also make sure that they are the correct size for the yarn you are using. For example, do not use large glass beads on a sportweight fabric because this will cause the knitting to sag. Make sure the hole in the center of the bead is big enough to pass a doubled end of yarn through.

Sequins

Sequins create an effect like fish scales on the knitted fabric and working with them is very much like working with beads. They are usually made of plastic, so avoid dry cleaning, pressing, or steaming them. Round sequins can be either flat or cupped—that is, the edges are faceted and tilt up toward the central hole. Take care when using the cupped variety that they face away from the surface of the knitting. As with beads, make sure that the hole in the sequin is large enough to accommodate a doubled end of yarn.

Other materials

The only other materials used in the projects in this book are:

- Petersham ribbon to strengthen the handles of the furry bag (project 4);
- Lining and eyelet trim for the pretty floral bag (project 15);
- Buttons for the buttoned fingerless gloves (project 14), driving gloves (project 20), and the beaded denim bag (project 25);
- Zipper for the summer coin purse (project 29).

All of these items can be purchased from good haberdashery stores.

15

Tools

Essentially, all you need is a pair of needles and, as long as they are the right size for the yarn you are using and the project you are making, you can start knitting. However, there are many other items of equipment that you may find useful.

CABLE NEEDLES

Needles

Needles are available in a variety of materials; the cheapest are aluminum and plastic. They can also be made from bamboo, steel, ebony, or even bone. Different materials will give you a different knitting experience, and personal preference will dictate which you choose to knit with. The important thing is that they are not bent and do not snag the yarn while knitting. The thickness or size of a needle should also be appropriate for the yarn you are using. A needle gauge is a handy and inexpensive tool to double-check the sizes of unmarked or old needles. There are three types of needle: straight, circular, and double pointed.

Straight needles

These come in pairs and vary from 10 to 18in (25 to 45cm) in length. Make sure that the needle you are using is long enough for the width of your project.

Circular needles

These are two short needle ends joined by a flexible plastic or nylon cord. They are handy for resting bulky or heavy projects in your lap or when the longest straight needle is not long enough for the item you are knitting, such as the dimple stitch shawl (project 30).

Double-pointed needles

These come in sets of four or five and are often used for knitting socks, gloves, and mittens in the round. They are also used when knitting i-cords, as featured in the pretty floral bag (project 15).

Cable needles

These short double-pointed needles are used to hold stitches at the back or front of the work while knitting cables, such as in the cabled mittens (project 18). Cranked cable needles have a V-shaped bend in them to stop stitches from slipping off when working the cable.

Stitch holders

These are used to hold stitches that have not been bound off so that they can be worked on later.

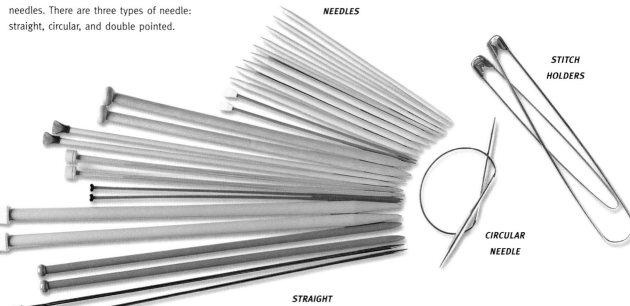

DOUBLE-POINTED NEEDLES

STITCH HOLDERS

CIRCULAR NEEDLE

STRAIGHT NEEDLES

POINT PROTECTORS

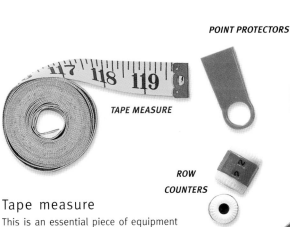

TAPE MEASURE

ROW COUNTERS

SCISSORS

BOBBINS

Tape measure
This is an essential piece of equipment for checking gauge and making sure your work is the correct size.

Row counter
Place this on the end of a needle and turn it after each row to keep count of the number of rows worked.

Glass-headed pins
Glass-headed dressmaking pins are used to hold pieces of knitted fabric at the correct size before pressing or steaming.

Stitch markers
These colored plastic or metal rings can be placed onto a needle or into a stitch to mark a particular stitch or row. You could use scraps of contrasting colored yarn tied into a slipknot instead.

Scissors
These are essential for trimming the ends of yarn, particularly at the back of work.

Sewing needles
Blunt yarn needles are ideal for weaving in ends and sewing seams. The eye should be large enough to thread the yarn through easily. Pointed sewing needles are useful for threading beads onto yarn, or sewing beads onto projects after knitting.

Crochet hook
This is handy for picking up dropped stitches and adding fringing to the edges of a piece of knitting.

Point protectors
Place these on the ends of needles when not in use to stop stitches from dropping off or to protect the tips of bamboo needles, which can chip or split.

Bobbins
These hold small quantities of yarn and are particularly useful when knitting intarsia.

Mohair brush
A mohair brush or teasel is useful for brushing up mohair after knitting to increase the hairiness of the fabric, such as the rainbow scarf (project 19).

Pompon maker
These come in various sizes and make it easier and quicker to create pompons for decorative touches.

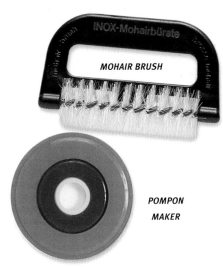

MOHAIR BRUSH

POMPON MAKER

GLASS-HEADED PINS

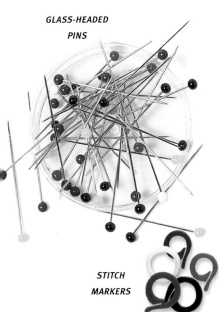

CROCHET HOOK

SEWING NEEDLES

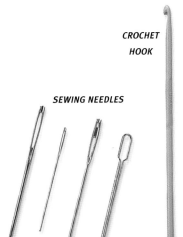

STITCH MARKERS

TIP: KEEPING A RECORD
It is worth keeping a sketchbook for making records of yarns used, dye lots, personal gauge, felting notes, and so on.

Getting started

When learning or practicing basic techniques, choose a medium yarn such as DK weight. This will help you feel that you are making some progress without having to work on too large a needle size.

Holding the yarn

There are numerous ways of holding the yarn; the best is the one that feels most comfortable. Those shown here leave your fingertips free to control the needles and tension the yarn so that it pulls quite tight as it passes through your hands.

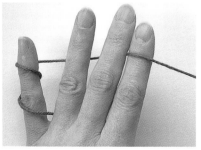

Right hand

Wrap the yarn around the little finger, then snake it over the ring finger, under the middle finger, and over the index finger.

Left hand

Holding the yarn in this hand is faster because the yarn does not have as far to travel to work each stitch. Wrap the yarn around the little finger, then snake it around the other fingers in a way that feels comfortable.

Holding the needles

Needles can be held from above, known as the "knife hold," or from beneath, known as the "pen hold." The left needle is always held from above, while the right needle can be held either way.

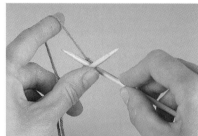
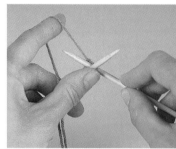

German method

This is the fastest method of knitting. Both the needles are held from above in the knife hold. The left hand controls the yarn and moves the stitches on the left needle, while the right hand moves the right needle into and out of the stitches on the left needle.

TIP: TAKE YOUR TIME

Before learning to knit, find a comfortable, quiet space that is well lit and relax—it should be an enjoyable experience. Make sure that the chair in which you are sitting supports your back and allows your arms to move freely. Allow yourself plenty of time to get to grips with the basics; everyone learns at a different speed, so the right pace is your pace.

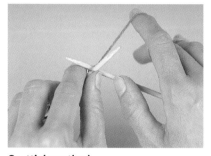

Scottish method

With this method, both needles are held from above in the knife hold. The left hand controls the needles, moving the stitches toward the tip of the left needle to be worked and guiding the right needle into and out of the stitches. The right hand controls the feed of the yarn.

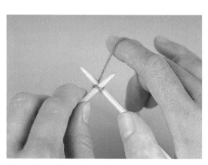

French method

Although considered to be more elegant than the German method and similar to the Scottish, this style of knitting is more time-consuming. The right needle is held from beneath in the pen hold between thumb and index finger. The right index finger is used to guide the yarn over the needles.

Casting on

All knitting starts with a foundation row called a cast-on and this begins with a stitch called a slipknot. There are various ways of casting on, some of which are best suited to certain stitches, but generally it is a matter of personal preference.

Making a slipknot

Make a slipknot and place it on the left needle to form the first cast-on stitch.

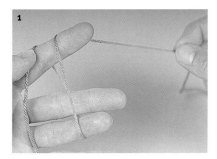

1 Make a loop by wrapping the yarn in a clockwise direction around the first three fingers of your left hand.

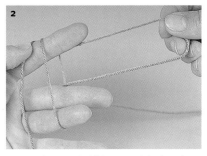

2 Pass the yarn held in your right hand under this loop to form another loop.

3 Remove your left hand from the first loop and pull the ends to tighten.

Cable cast-on

This popular cast-on method uses two needles and creates a cabled effect along the cast-on edge.

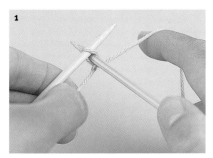

1 Make a slipknot and place it on the left needle. Insert the tip of the right needle into the slipknot from front to back.

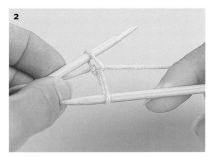

2 Wrap the yarn counterclockwise around the tip of the right needle. Pull the right needle back through the slipknot, drawing the yarn through the slipknot to make a new stitch.

4 Place the loop from your right hand onto the needle and tighten. Do not pull too tight.

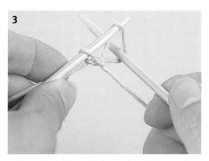

3 Transfer this stitch from the right needle to the left.

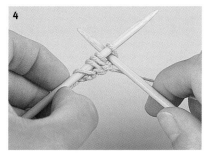

4 Use the same process to make as many stitches as required, but from now on insert the tip of the right needle between the top two stitches on the left needle. Transfer each new stitch to the left needle as before.

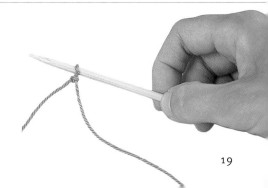

Knit and purl

All knitted fabrics, no matter how complicated or simple, are based on two stitches: knit and purl. Always hold the yarn at the back of the work for a knit stitch and at the front of the work for a purl stitch unless instructed otherwise in the pattern (yb indicates that you should take the yarn to the back of the work, yf indicates that you should bring the yarn to the front of the work).

Knit stitch

Cast on the required number of stitches and hold the yarn at the back of the work. As you work across a row, the stitches will move from the left to the right needle. At the end of the row, swap the needles so that the needle with the stitches is in your left hand and the empty needle is in your right hand, ready to work the next row.

1 Insert the tip of the right needle into the stitch on the left needle from front to back.

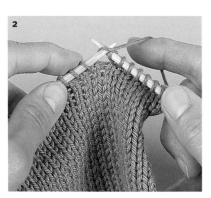

2 Wrap the yarn counterclockwise around the tip of the right needle.

3 Use the right needle to pull the wrapped yarn through the stitch on the left needle to create a new stitch on the right needle. Slip the original stitch off the left needle.

Purl stitch

Cast on the required number of stitches and hold the yarn at the front of the work. As with knit stitch, swap the needles when you reach the end of the row.

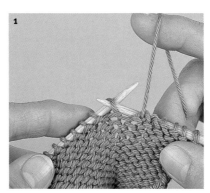

1 Insert the tip of the right needle into the stitch on the left needle from back to front.

2 Wrap the yarn counterclockwise around the tip of the right needle.

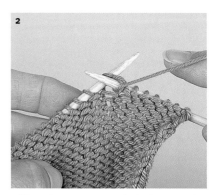

3 Use the right needle to pull the wrapped yarn through the stitch on the left needle to create a new stitch on the right needle. Slip the original stitch off the left needle.

TIP: COUNTING ROWS

When you swap the needles at the end of each row, mark off the row you have just finished in the pattern or use a row counter to keep count of where you are.

Stitch patterns

Different combinations of knit and purl stitches produce different types of knitted fabric.

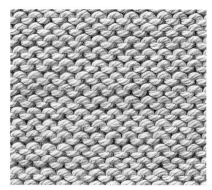

Garter stitch

Garter stitch is the simplest stitch pattern because it is created by either knitting or purling all the stitches on every row. The fabric it produces is springy and dense in texture and when pressed remains flat. This makes it ideal for use on edges.

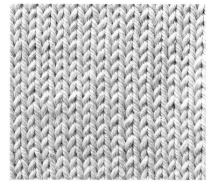

Stockinette stitch

Stockinette stitch is created by alternating knit and purl rows. This produces a more noticeable difference between the front or knit side, which is smooth, and the back or purl side, which has a more ridged appearance.

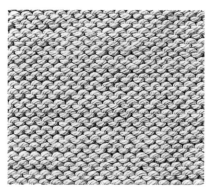

Reverse stockinette stitch

This is the same as stockinette stitch but uses the ridged purl side as the right side of the fabric.

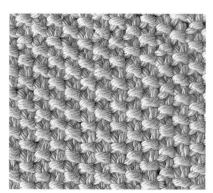

Seed stitch

This is created by alternating knit and purl stitches on one row, but on the next row working knit on top of knit stitches and purl on top of purl stitches. The fabric created is firm in texture like garter stitch and remains flat after pressing.

TIP: RIGHT SIDE/WRONG SIDE

Strictly speaking, the right and wrong side of the fabric depends on the stitch pattern you are using. With stockinette stitch, for example, the right side is the smooth face of the fabric and the ridged surface is the wrong side. However, in the case of garter stitch, both sides are the same. All of the patterns in this book tell you which side is the right side for each project.

Ribbing

Ribbing is characteristically vertical fabric created by alternating knit and purl stitches on one row and then purling on top of the stitches knitted on the previous row and vice versa. Due to its elastic nature, it is often used as a means of edging knitted fabrics.

TIP: JOINING NEW YARN

Whenever a ball of yarn is about to run out, join a new one at the beginning of a row. Avoid joining a new ball of yarn halfway through a row. To help keep good tension when starting a new yarn, tie it around the original yarn (the knot can be undone when you are weaving in the ends of yarn after you have finished the piece). Without breaking off the yarn used for the previous row, tie the new yarn around the end of the old yarn, leaving a tail about 6in (15cm) long. Slide the knot up to the next stitch and work the row using the new yarn. Hold the tail of the yarn out of the way for the first few stitches.

Binding off

Binding off is a neat way of giving knitted fabrics a finished edge that will not unravel. There are various ways of binding off and each creates a different effect. It is also possible to make a decorative feature of binding off by using a contrasting colored yarn.

Binding off knitwise

This is the most common technique for binding off and is sometimes called "chain bind-off" because it makes a chain along the top of the knitting.

2 Lift this stitch over the second stitch and slip it off the right needle so that you have only 1 stitch on the right needle.

1 Knit the first 2 stitches from the left needle onto the right needle in the usual way. * With the yarn at the back of the work, insert the tip of the left needle into the first of these knitted stitches.

3 Knit the next stitch on the left needle so that there are 2 stitches on the right needle once again. Repeat from * until you reach the last stitch. Break off the yarn, pull the end of the yarn through the last stitch, and tighten.

3 Purl the next stitch on the left needle so that there are 2 stitches on the right needle once again. Repeat from * until you reach the last stitch. Break off the yarn, pull the end of the yarn through the last stitch, and tighten.

2 Lift this stitch over the second stitch and slip it off the right needle so that you have only 1 stitch on the right needle.

Binding off purlwise

1 Purl the first 2 stitches from the left needle onto the right needle in the usual way. * With the yarn at the front of the work, insert the tip of the left needle into the first of these purled stitches.

TIP: DROPPED STITCHES

If you drop any stitches, pick them up as soon as you notice and before binding off. With the knit side of the work facing you, insert a crochet hook into the dropped stitch from the front. Pick up the first horizontal bar of unraveled yarn above the dropped stitch and pull it through the stitch to the front. Continue doing this until all the unraveled bars have been picked up, turning the work so that the knit side is facing you if necessary. Transfer the stitch back onto the left knitting needle when you have finished.

Binding off in pattern

Sometimes a pattern will instruct you to bind off in pattern. This means that you should bind off all knit stitches knitwise and all purl stitches purlwise. For example, if the pattern is double ribbing, as shown here, bind off the first 2 stitches knitwise, the next 2 stitches purlwise, and so on.

Three-needle bind-off

This is a method of binding off two sets of stitches together. This creates an invisible seam if the two sets of stitches are bound off with right sides facing, or can be made into a decorative feature when the stitches are bound off with wrong sides facing.

1 If you are joining two separate pieces of knitting together, place both needles in your left hand with the appropriate sides of the work facing each other. If you need to join two halves of a single piece of knitting together—such as the bright beaded mittens (project 2)—work as instructed by the pattern for the first half of the stitches, then turn the right needle so that the appropriate sides of the fabric are facing and both needles are in your left hand.

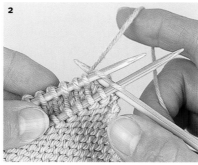

2 Insert the tip of a third needle through the first stitch on both needles in your left hand. Work these 2 stitches together.

3 Work the next pair of stitches together, then use one of the needles in your left hand to lift the first stitch over the second stitch on the right needle, letting it drop off the end of the right needle. When you reach the last pair of stitches, break off the yarn, pull the end of the yarn through both stitches, and tighten.

TIP: NEATENING THE LAST STITCH

The last bound-off stitch is sometimes considerably larger than the others. This can be neatened by sewing it into the seam when joining pieces together. If this is not possible, bind off all the stitches except the last one. Slip this stitch onto the right needle. Use the tip of the left needle to pick up the final stitch on the row below, then return the slipped stitch to the left needle. Work these 2 stitches together.

Patterns and charts

The instructions for knitting a project may be provided in either written or chart form. Always read the whole pattern before you start knitting to ensure that you have everything you need and understand all the instructions.

Essential information

All patterns provide a list containing the size of the finished item, the materials and tools required, the gauge of the piece, and the abbreviations used in the instructions. Although many abbreviations are standardized, such as k for knit and p for purl, some of them vary, so always read the abbreviations before you start knitting.

Abbreviations

The abbreviations used in this book are:

b1	place 1 bead
beg	beginning
c6b	cable 6 back
c6f	cable 6 forward
foll	following
inc	increase/increasing
k	knit
k1b	knit 1 stitch together with stitch in row below
k1w	knit 1 stitch (or more if specified) by wrapping yarn twice around needle
k2tog	knit 2 stitches together (or more if specified)
m1	make 1 stitch (or more if specified)
p	purl
p2tog	purl 2 stitches together (or more if specified)
patt	pattern
rem	remaining
rep	repeat
rs	right side
seq 1	place 1 sequin
skpo	slip 1 stitch, knit 1 stitch, pass slipped stitch over knitted stitch
sl	slip specified number of stitches from left to right needle without working them
st(s)	stitch(es)
tbl	through back of loop
ws	wrong side
y2rn	wrap yarn twice around needle
yb	take yarn back
yf	bring yarn forward

Repeats

When following pattern instructions, you will find that some of them appear within parentheses and some are marked with an asterisk. Along with the use of abbreviations, these help to shorten the amount of space needed for each pattern. Instructions that appear within parentheses are to be repeated. For example, instead of writing "p2, k2, p2, k2, p2, k2," the pattern will simply say "(p2, k2) 3 times." Asterisks (*) and other symbols (such as +) mark whole sets of instructions within a pattern that are to be repeated. For example, "repeat from * to **" means repeat the instructions between the single asterisk and the double asterisks.

Gauge

Gauge is extremely important because it can mean the difference between the failure or success of a project. Simply put, it is the number of stitches and rows measured over a 4in (10cm) square. It is always advisable to knit a small swatch to measure your gauge and compare it to that stated in the pattern. The instructions will indicate what type of stitch pattern the gauge has been measured over. Your swatch should be knitted in the same stitch with the appropriate yarn and needles.

You may feel that knitting a test swatch is a waste of time but remember that it could well save you from reknitting or abandoning a project or being disappointed with the end result. Knitting is an individual craft—we do not all knit to the same gauge.

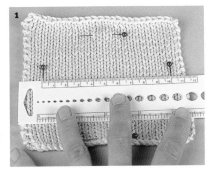

Measuring gauge

1 Using a ruler, measure 4in (10cm) horizontally and vertically across your gauge swatch and mark these dimensions with pins.

2 Use the tip of a knitting needle to count the number of stitches and rows between the pins. If you find that you have more stitches and rows than the pattern suggests, your gauge is too tight and you should use larger needles. If you have fewer stitches and rows, your knitting is too loose and you should use smaller needles. Knit another test swatch and check that it matches the gauge in the pattern.

Reading charts

Charts are a graphic representation of your knitting. Each square represents a stitch, and each horizontal line of squares is a row. All graphs have a key nearby to explain each of the symbols and/or colors used. When reading the charts in this book, start at the bottom right corner and read from right to left for right side rows that are numbered down the right edge of the chart. Read from left to right for wrong side rows that are numbered down the left edge.

TIP: ENLARGING CHARTS

If you are new to working from charts, you may find it helpful to enlarge them on a photocopier to make them easier to follow. It is also a good idea to mark off each row as you go.

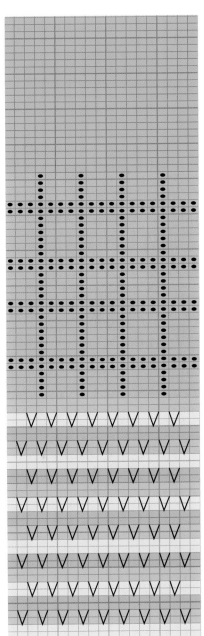

KEY

▓	Red yarn
▓	Purple yarn
▓	Pink yarn
▓	Green yarn
☐	K on rs, p on ws
●	P on rs, k on ws
V	Sl st knitwise on rs, purlwise on ws

This example of a chart and key is from the patchwork bag on page 62. You can see the knitted strip in the center of the photograph to the left of the chart.

Increasing

There are lots of different ways of increasing the number of stitches in order to shape your knitting either gradually (single stitch increasing) or more drastically (multiple stitch increasing).

Increase 1 knitwise

This increase can be worked anywhere on a row and involves knitting into a stitch twice in order to make an extra stitch.

Increase 1 purlwise

This increase can be worked anywhere on a row and involves purling into a stitch twice in order to make an extra stitch.

Make 1 knitwise

This increase uses the horizontal bar that lies between pairs of stitches to create a new stitch. It can be worked anywhere on a row.

1 Work to the point in the row where you need to increase. Knit into the front of the stitch on the left needle in the usual way, but do not slip it off the left needle when you have finished.

1 Work to the point in the row where you need to increase. Purl into the front of the stitch on the left needle in the usual way, but do not slip it off the left needle when you have finished.

1 Work to the point where you need to increase. Insert the tip of the right needle underneath the horizontal bar lying between the last stitch on the right needle and the first stitch on the left needle.

2 Keeping the original stitch on the left needle and the yarn at the back of the work, knit into the back of the stitch— you have now increased 1 stitch. Slip the stitch from the left needle.

2 Keeping the original stitch on the left needle and the yarn at the front of the work, purl into the back of the stitch— you have now increased 1 stitch. Slip the stitch from the left needle.

2 Lift this bar and slip it onto the left needle. Knit into the back of this loop to create a new stitch, slipping the lifted loop off the left needle when you have finished.

Make 2 knitwise

This is basically the same as make 1 knitwise except that you are working into both the back and front of the loop to create 2 new stitches.

1

1 Repeat steps 1 and 2 of make 1 knitwise but do not slip the lifted loop off the left needle at the end.

2

2 Now insert the right needle into the front of the loop and knit the stitch. You have now made 2 new stitches. Slip the loop off the left needle.

Make 1 purlwise

This increase is worked anywhere on a row and again uses the horizontal bar that lies between pairs of stitches to create a new stitch. Repeat steps 1 and 2 of make 1 knitwise, but purl into the back of the lifted loop instead of knitting into it.

Make 2 purlwise

Follow the instructions for make 1 purlwise but do not slip the lifted loop off the left needle after you have purled into the back of it. Now insert the right needle into the front of the loop and purl the stitch. You have now made 2 new stitches. Slip the loop off the left needle.

TIP: HOLDING STITCHES

Some projects require stitches to be left on a holder to be worked at a later stage in the pattern. Simply insert the pin of the holder from right to left through each stitch, taking care not to twist them. When you need to work on these stitches, slip them from the holder onto a knitting needle, again taking care not to twist them.

TIP: TURNING ROWS

Some projects require you to turn the needles part way through a row in order to shape the knitting. This technique, also known as short-row shaping, is used to create the vent in the rainbow scarf (project 19), the heels on socks (projects 5 and 17), and thumbs and fingers on gloves and mittens (projects 2, 8, 14, 18, and 20).

Cable increase

It is sometimes necessary to increase multiple stitches at the beginning of a row. This technique is essentially the same as the cable cast-on.

1

1 Work to the point in the pattern where you need to increase. Insert the tip of the right needle between the first and second stitches on the left needle.

2

2 Wrap the yarn counterclockwise around the tip of the right needle. Pull the right needle back, drawing the loop of yarn between the two stitches. Transfer this new stitch onto the left needle. Repeat this process until you have the required number of increased stitches.

Decreasing

As with increasing, there are numerous methods of decreasing in order to shape a piece of knitting, either gradually by knitting stitches together or more severely by binding stitches off.

Knitting stitches together

This can be used anywhere on a row to knit 2 or more stitches together. The examples shown here demonstrate 2 stitches being knit together in order to decrease 1 stitch.

K2tog

Knit 2 together creates a slope to the right on the face of the fabric.

1 Work to where you need to decrease. Insert the tip of the right needle knitwise into the front of the first 2 stitches on the left needle.

2 Knit the 2 stitches together as if they were a single stitch. You have now decreased 1 stitch.

K2tog tbl

Knit 2 together through the back of the loop creates a slope to the left on the face of the fabric.

1 Work to where you need to decrease. Insert the tip of the right needle knitwise into the back of the first 2 stitches on the left needle.

2 Knit the 2 stitches together as if they were a single stitch. You have now decreased 1 stitch.

Purling stitches together

This can be used anywhere on a row to purl 2 or more stitches together. The examples shown here demonstrate 2 stitches being purled together in order to decrease 1 stitch.

P2tog

Purl 2 together creates a slope to the right on the face of the fabric.

1 Work to where you need to decrease. Insert the tip of the right needle purlwise into the front of the first 2 stitches on the left needle.

2 Purl the 2 stitches together as if they were a single stitch. You have now decreased 1 stitch.

P2tog tbl

Purl 2 together through the back of the loop creates a slope to the left on the face of the fabric.

1 Work to where you need to decrease. Insert the tip of the right needle purlwise into the back of the first 2 stitches on the left needle.

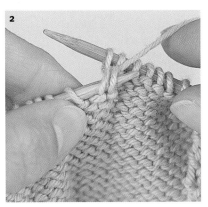

2 Purl the 2 stitches as if they were a single stitch. You have now decreased 1 stitch.

Slip stitch decreasing

Skpo (slip 1, knit 1, pass slipped stitch over) is a method of decreasing that is often used when making lace holes. It creates a slope to the left on the face of the fabric.

1 Insert the tip of the right needle knitwise into the first stitch on the left needle and slip the stitch from the left to the right needle without working it.

2 Knit the next stitch on the left needle in the usual way, then insert the tip of the left needle into the slipped stitch on the right needle. Lift the slipped stitch over the knitted stitch and drop it off the right needle.

Bind-off decrease

This decrease is usually done at the beginning of a row. Simply work to where you need to decrease, then bind off the number of stitches required by the pattern in the usual way. If you are instructed to do it in the middle of a row, you will need to rejoin the yarn to the stitches before the bind-off in order to continue working them.

TIP: FULLY FASHIONED SHAPING

Visible shaping, where the increases and decreases are worked a few stitches in from the edges of the knitting, is called fully fashioned shaping. Working into the front or back of stitches that are knitted or purled together emphasizes the way the knitting is shaped or "fashioned," and many of the projects in this book use this as a decorative feature.

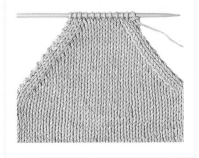

Other stitch techniques

*Having covered the basics of knitting, purling, increasing, and decreasing,
you will find that there are many variations on these instructions used
in knitting patterns to create specific effects.*

Slipping stitches

Many techniques involve slipping stitches
from one needle to another without
working them.

Drop stitches

These are formed by wrapping the yarn twice around the right needle instead of once, and
dropping the extra loop on the following row. This technique is always done knitwise in
this book and is used for 1, 2, or 5 stitches at a time (abbreviated as k1w, k2w, or k5w).

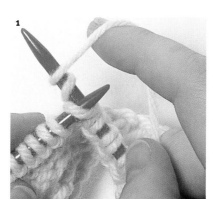

1 Knit the next stitch, wrapping the yarn
around the needle twice.

3 On the following row, work the double
loop as instructed in the pattern,
allowing the extra loop to drop from the
left needle as you do so.

Knitwise

To slip a stitch knitwise, insert the tip
of the right needle into the stitch on the
left needle as if to knit it. Slip the stitch
from the left to the right needle without
working into it.

Lace holes

As well as slip stitch decreasing (see page
29), there are several methods of creating
decorative lace holes in a piece of knitting.

2 Pull the double loop through as you
complete the knit stitch.

Purlwise

To slip a stitch purlwise, insert the tip
of the right needle into the stitch on the
left needle as if to purl it. Slip the stitch
from the left to the right needle without
working into it.

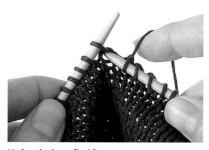

Knit 1 below (k1b)

With the yarn at the back of the work,
insert the tip of the right needle into the
stitch one row below the next stitch on
the left needle. Knit this stitch and the
one above together as if they were a
single stitch.

Yarn overs

This involves taking the yarn over the right needle to create a lace hole. Depending on the next stitch, the pattern will instruct you to bring the yarn forward (yf) or take the yarn back (yb) so that you have to wrap the yarn over the needle to make the next stitch, thereby creating the hole.

1 This example shows a yarn over between 2 knit stitches. Instead of knitting the second stitch with the yarn at the back of the work in the usual way, the yarn was brought forward between the needles to the front of the work, then wrapped over the right needle to knit the stitch.

2 This yarn over is between 2 purl stitches. Instead of purling the second stitch with the yarn at the front of the work in the usual way, the yarn was taken between the needles to the back of the work, then wrapped over the right needle to purl the stitch.

Picking up stitches

Picking up stitches enables you to add an edge or border to a finished piece of knitted fabric. If rushed, it can easily spoil a project, so relax and take your time.

Along a vertical edge

When picking up stitches along a vertical edge, work with the right side of the fabric facing you. These stitches can be fairly tight, so you may find it helpful to use a smaller sized needle for picking up and then change to the size required for knitting the edge.

1 Insert a needle from front to back between the first two stitches of the first row—that is, one whole stitch in from the edge.

2 Wrap the yarn around the needle and pull the needle to the front of the work, drawing a loop of yarn through at the same time. You have now created a new stitch. Continue in this way along the knitted edge until you have the required number of stitches.

Along a horizontal edge

When picking up stitches along a horizontal edge, work into the center of the stitch below the bind-off edge or directly above the cast-on edge. Again, you may find it helpful to pick up using a slightly smaller needle.

1 Insert the right needle from front to back through the center of the stitch.

2 Wrap the yarn around the needle and pull to the front of the work, drawing a loop of yarn through to create a new stitch. Do this for as many stitches as required.

Color work

Working with color adds a new dimension to plain knitting and presents endless possibilities when creating your own accessories. The simplest way to introduce color is to work in stripes. It is also possible to work with more than one color in a row by using intarsia or fairisle techniques.

Stripes

Knitting horizontal stripes is a quick and easy way to add color to a project and produces a single weight of fabric. You can break off and join the yarns for each stripe, or carry them up the side of the work. Avoid pulling the yarns too tightly when carrying them up the side because this can cause the edge to distort.

1

1 Insert the right needle into the first stitch. Lay the second yarn (orange) across the first yarn (pink) and work the next stitch with the second yarn.

2

2 Catch in the unused yarn (pink) on every other row by lying it across the yarn currently in use (orange) before working the first stitch of the new row.

Intarsia

Intarsia uses a separate length of yarn for each area of colored knitting. This creates a single thickness of fabric because there are no yarns carried across the back of the work. Twisting the different yarns where they meet means there are no holes.

1

Joining a new color

1 Insert the right needle into the next stitch on the left needle. Making sure the tail end of the first color (pink) is on the left, place the new yarn (green) over the first yarn and between the two needles.

2

2 Bring the new yarn up from under the first yarn and work the next stitch, moving the tail end off the needle as you go.

Changing colors on a knit row

Work to where you need to change color. Insert the tip of the right needle into the next stitch knitwise. Bring the first color (pink) over the top of the second color (yellow) and drop. Now pick up the second color. Making sure the colors stay twisted, continue as directed by the pattern.

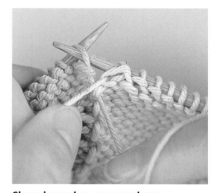

Changing colors on a purl row

Work to where you need to change color. Insert the tip of the right needle into the next stitch purlwise. Bring the first color (yellow) over the top of the second color (pink) and drop, then pick up the second color. Making sure the colors stay twisted, continue as directed by the pattern.

TIP: USING BOBBINS

Bobbins are used when you do not want to have whole balls of different colored yarns hanging off your work. They can be bought readymade or you can make your own.

1 Wrap the yarn around the thumb and little finger of your hand in a figure-eight shape.

2 To finish off, remove from your hand and wind the loose end of the yarn around the center to secure. Use the yarn from the center when knitting.

Fairisle

Fairisle is a method of knitting where different colors are carried across the back of the work, producing a double thickness fabric. Take care because the knitted fabric can pucker if the yarns are pulled too tightly across the back. There are two methods of carrying the yarns—twisting and stranding.

Twisting

This method is used when a color needs to be carried more than 3 stitches across the back of the knitting. The yarns are caught or twisted in every second or third stitch.

1 Work in yarn A (pink) for 2 or 3 stitches. Take yarn B (yellow) from under yarn A and wrap it clockwise over the tip of the right needle and left forefinger.

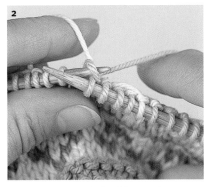

2 Work the next stitch with yarn A, dropping yarn B from the left needle as you do so. You have just twisted in yarn B.

3 Continue working with yarn A in this way, holding yarn B at the back of the work with your left forefinger until you need to twist it in again.

Stranding

This method allows a color to be carried across the back of the knitting without being caught in by the other colors used. Ideally, not more than 3 stitches should be worked between color changes because this can cause long loops to form on the reverse of the work. These are known as "floats" and can easily snag when the item is used.

1 Using yarn A (pink), work 3 stitches. Drop yarn A and pick up yarn B (yellow), carrying it over yarn A. Work the next 3 stitches, then drop yarn B.

2 Pick up yarn A from underneath yarn B, bring it across the back of the last 3 stitches, and work the next 3 stitches. Continue in this way, keeping the stitches on the needles spread out so that the carried yarn is not pulled too taut.

Finishing

Now that you have completed your project, you have come to the task that a lot of knitters hate—weaving in ends, pressing, and sewing seams. Having knitted your accessories with such care, take your time. There are many finishing tips and techniques; the ones described here will help you with the projects in this book.

Weaving in ends

Yarn ends are left whenever you change color, join a new ball, or sew seams. Always leave a tail end of yarn about 6in (15cm) long so that you can weave it neatly into the knitting. Undo any knots joining yarns, then thread the yarn end through a blunt-pointed yarn needle.

2 Take the needle back, catching in the woven-in yarn for 2–3 stitches. Stretch the knitting widthwise and trim the end of the yarn.

1 Check your pattern for the finished measurements. Using large glass-headed pins and with the wrong side of the knitting facing upward, pin the pieces out to the correct dimensions, taking care not to stretch the knitting out of shape.

Along a seam

Run the needle in and out of the stitches inside the seam at the edge of the knitting for about 3in (8cm). Pull the yarn through and trim the end.

Along a row

1 Run the needle in and out of the back of stitches of the same color, working along the row for about 4–6 stitches.

Blocking and pressing

Blocking is the term used for pinning out each knitted piece to the correct size before pressing. You can use an ironing board for small pieces or make a blocking board by placing a thin layer of batting on top of a sheet of hardboard. Cover this with a piece of checked fabric stretched tautly and pinned or taped securely to the hardboard. The checks will help you to lay the work straight.

2 Place a damp cloth over the fabric and press with an iron set at the correct temperature for the yarn used. Do not apply too much pressure or you will flatten the texture of the knitting. For cabled or highly textured pieces, hold a steam iron about 1–2in (2–4cm) above the surface and allow the steam to penetrate the fabric. Avoid pressing or steaming ribbing because this causes it to lose elasticity.

Sewing seams

There are several methods of sewing seams together. Overcasting, backstitch, blanket stitch, and chain stitch are used in this book. Use a yarn needle and matching colored yarn for the first two (contrasting yarn is used here for clarity), and either matching or contrasting yarn for the latter.

Blanket stitch

This stitch can be used as a decorative way of finishing edges and joining seams. Working about ¼in (5mm) from the edge, take the needle from front to back through the fabric. Move the needle 1 stitch along the edge, then thread from front to back. Point the needle up, catching the yarn around it, and pull through. Continue along the whole seam.

Chain stitch

This stitch can be used as a decorative edging or seam. Bring the needle through to the front of the knitting, then take it to the back again at the same point where you brought it to the front, creating a loop of yarn. Bring the needle to the front a short distance farther along and through the center of the loop. Tighten and repeat.

Backstitch

This creates a strong, firm seam. Take extra care on items such as hats when the seam will be more noticeable.

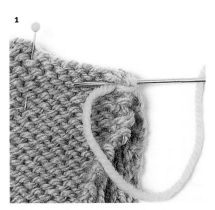

1 Hold the pieces right sides together, pinning them if you wish, and secure the yarn at one end of the seam with a couple of small overlapping stitches.

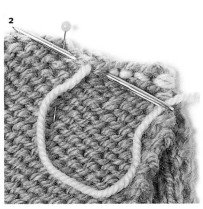

2 Insert the needle through both knitted pieces from front to back 1 stitch along from where you started. * Take it across the back of the work for about 2 stitches, then bring the needle through to the front of the fabric again. Insert the needle into the work where it first went in and repeat from *, pulling the thread flat against the seam as you go. Take care not to pull too tightly. Secure the yarn at the other end of the seam with a couple of overlapping stitches, then weave in both ends.

Overcasting

This is sometimes referred to as a flat seam because it produces a very narrow seam. Hold the edges of both pieces right sides together in one hand. With your other hand, insert the needle from the back of the work through the edge stitches of both pieces. Pull the yarn through to the front, then take it over the knitted edge and sew once again a few stitches along from where you started. Continue evenly along the edge and secure at both ends by weaving in the yarn ends.

TIP: AFTERCARE

Always refer to the instructions on the yarn ball band for guidelines as to washing or dry cleaning (if you are not going to keep the ball band, transfer the information to your sketchbook). Beaded and sequinned projects should be hand washed with care. Use lukewarm water and a suitable detergent, try not to agitate the item too much, and avoid wringing because this can stretch it out of shape or damage the beads and sequins. Gently squeeze out the excess water by placing the item on a towel and applying light pressure. Felted items, although already shrunk, should be hand washed to avoid additional shrinkage.

quick & easy projects

THIS CHAPTER CONTAINS 30 PROJECTS THAT ARE QUICK AND EASY TO KNIT,

RANGING FROM HATS, SCARVES, AND GLOVES TO BAGS, SOCKS, AND SHAWLS. AT

THE BEGINNING OF EACH PROJECT YOU WILL FIND A LIST OF THE MATERIALS AND

NEEDLES YOU WILL NEED, PLUS THE GAUGE AND ABBREVIATIONS USED IN THAT

PARTICULAR PATTERN. THERE ARE ALSO TIPS AND STEP-BY-STEP INSTRUCTIONS

FOR ANY NEW SKILLS THAT ARE REQUIRED TO COMPLETE EACH PROJECT.

Project 1: Chunky ribbed scarf

This scarf is worked in a drop-stitch ribbing texture that knits up quickly using a beautifully soft angora/merino mix yarn. Using larger needles and doubled yarn for the end panels of the scarf creates a fabric that looks heavy but is actually very light to wear.

before you start

Measurements   8¼in (21cm) wide x 67¾in (172cm) long

Materials   4 x 2oz (50g) balls (approx. 120yds/110m per ball) bulky-weight angora/extra fine merino mix yarn

Needles   1 pair size 10½ (6.5mm) needles
1 pair size 17 (12mm) needles

Gauge   **Using yarn single**—18 sts x 23 rows to 4in (10cm) measured over pattern using size 10½ (6.5mm) needles
Using yarn doubled—10 sts x 13 rows to 4in (10cm) measured over pattern using size 17 (12mm) needles

Abbreviations   inc 1—increase 1 stitch by purling into front and back of next stitch; k—knit; k1w/k2w—knit 1 or 2 stitches by wrapping yarn twice around needle for each stitch; k2tog/k3tog—knit 2 or 3 stitches together; m1—make 1 stitch by picking up horizontal bar before next stitch, putting it onto left needle, then knitting into back of it; p—purl; p2tog—purl 2 stitches together; patt—pattern; rep—repeat; rs—right side; sl—slip stitch purlwise from left to right needle without working it; st(s)—stitch(es); tbl—through back of loop; ws—wrong side; yb—take yarn back between needles; yf—bring yarn forward between needles

Knitting the scarf
Using size 17 (12mm) needles and two ends of yarn, cast on 23 sts.

First end panel ribbing
Row 1 (rs): K1, p1, *k1, p2, rep from * to last 3 sts, k1, p1, k1.
Row 2: *K2, p1, rep from * to last 2 sts, k2.
Row 3: K1, p1, *k1w, p2, k1, p2, rep from * to last 3 sts, k1w, p1, k1.
Row 4: *K2, yf, sl 1 dropping extra loop, yb, k2, p1, rep from * to last 5 sts, k2, yf, sl 1 dropping extra loop, yb, k2.
Row 5: K1, p1, yb, sl 1, yf, p2, k1, p2, rep from * to last 3 sts, yb, sl 1, yf, p1, k1.
Row 6: *K2, yf, sl 1, yb, k2, p1, rep from * to last 5 sts, k2, yf, sl 1, yb, k2.

Rows 7–33: Repeat rows 3–6 until 33 rows have been completed.
Break off one end of yarn, change to size 10½ (6.5mm) needles, and continue working with a single end of yarn.
Row 34 (increase row): *K1, m1, k1, inc 1, rep from * to last 2 sts, k1, m1, k1 (38 sts).

Center ribbing
Row 35: *K2, p2, (k2w, p2) twice, rep from * to last 2 sts, k2.
Row 36: K1, p1, *(k2, yf, sl 2 dropping extra loops, yb) twice, k2, p2, rep from * to last 4 sts, k2, p1, k1.
Row 37: *K2, p2, (yb, sl 2, yf, p2) twice, rep from * to last 2 sts, k2.
Row 38: K1, p1, *(k2, yf, sl 2, yb) twice, k2, p2, rep from * to last 4 sts, k2, p1, k1.
Continue in patt as established by rows 35–38 until scarf measures 55in (140cm) from cast-on edge, finishing after row 37 with ws facing for decrease row.
Decrease row: K3tog tbl, *(k1, p2tog) twice, (p1, k2tog) twice, rep from * to last 11 sts, (k1, p2tog) twice, p2tog, k3tog (23 sts).
Break off single yarn.

Second end panel ribbing
Changing back to size 17 (12mm) needles and using doubled yarn, work rows 1–33 of the first end panel ribbing. Bind off ribwise.

Finishing
Weave in the ends and steam the scarf gently on the wrong side, taking care not to flatten the texture.

The beauty of
this scarf lies in
its texture, created
by using doubled
yarn, drop stitches,
and ribbing.

Project 2: Bright beaded mittens

Just the thing to brighten dreary cold mornings, these mittens use an easy beading technique to produce embellished detail that looks much more difficult to create than it really is. The finger section and cuff are studded with decorative beads, and simple knit and purl stitching in four different colors creates a funky striped effect.

before you start

Measurements	One size to fit average-sized woman's hands
Materials	2oz (50g) balls (approx. 123yds/113m per ball) DK merino/cotton mix yarn in 4 colors:

Yarn A Brown x 1 ball   **Yarn B** Crimson x 1 ball
Yarn C Orange x 1 ball   **Yarn D** Maroon x 1 ball
170 small bronze beads

Needles	1 pair size 3 (3mm) needles
	3 size 5 (3.75mm) needles
Gauge	24 sts x 30 rows to 4in (10cm) measured over stockinette stitch using size 5 (3.75mm) needles
Abbreviations	b1—place 1 bead; inc 1—increase 1 stitch by knitting into front and back of next stitch; k—knit; k2tog—knit 2 stitches together; m1—make 1 stitch by picking horizontal bar before next stitch, putting it onto left needle, then knitting into back of it; p—purl; rs—right side; st(s)—stitch(es); tbl—through back of loop; ws—wrong side

TIP: WORKING THE STRIPE PATTERN

Do not break off yarns when working the stripe pattern at the wrist of the mittens. Instead, carry the yarns not in use up the side of the mittens. This reduces the number of ends to be woven in afterward.

TIP: NEVER LOSE YOUR PLACE

Instead of buying markers, you can make them from scraps of contrasting colored yarn tied in a slipknot.

Knitting the mittens
RIGHT MITTEN

Using size 3 (3mm) needles and yarn A threaded with 20 beads, cast on 41 sts.

Row 1 (rs): K1, (b1, k1) to end.
Row 2: K1, (p1, k1) to end.
Row 3: Using yarn B, p1, (k1, p1) to end.
Row 4: Using yarn B, k1, (p1, k1) to end.
Row 5: Using yarn C, p1, (k1, p1) to end.
Row 6: Using yarn D, k1, (p1, k1) to end.
Row 7: Using yarn D, p1, (k1, p1) to end.
Row 8: Using yarn A, k1, (p1, k1) to end.
Row 9: Using yarn A, p1, (k1, p1) to end.
Row 10: Using yarn C, k1, (p1, k1) to end.
Row 11: Using yarn B, p1, (k1, p1) to end.
Row 12: Using yarn D, k1, (p1, k1) to end.
Row 13: Using yarn A, p1, (k1, p1) to end.
Row 14: Using yarn B, k1, (p1, k1) to end.
Row 15: Using yarn B, p1, (k1, p1) to end.
Row 16: Using yarn C, k1, (p1, k1) to end.
Row 17: Using yarn D, p1, (k1, p1) to end.
Row 18: Using yarn D, k1, (p1, k1) to end.
Row 19: Using yarn A, p1, (k1, p1) to end.
Row 20: Using yarn B, (k1, p1) to last st, inc 1 (42 sts).
Change to size 5 (3.75mm) needles, break off all yarns except yarn B, and continue working with yarn B only.
Row 21: (P1, k1) to end.
Row 22: P all sts.

Shaping the thumb gusset

Row 23 (rs): K22, place marker on needle, m1, k1, m1, place marker on needle, k19 (44 sts).
Row 24 and all ws rows: P all sts.
Row 25: K all sts.

Row 27: K to marker, slip marker onto right needle, m1, k to next marker, m1, slip marker onto right needle, k to end (46 sts).
Row 29: K all sts.
Row 31: K to marker, slip marker onto right needle, m1, k to next marker, m1, slip marker onto right needle, k to end (48 sts).
Row 33: K all sts.
Row 35: K to marker, slip marker onto right needle, m1, k to next marker, m1, slip marker onto right needle, k to end (50 sts).
Row 37: K all sts.
Row 39: K32 and turn.

Knitting the thumb

Next row (ws): P11, turn, and cast on 3 sts.
Next row (rs): Beginning with a k row, work 12 rows in stockinette stitch on these 14 sts only.

Shaping top of thumb

Next row (rs): K2, (k2tog, k1) 4 times (10 sts).
Next row: P all sts.
Next row: (K2tog) 5 times.
Break off yarn B, making sure you leave enough to sew the seam, and thread the yarn through remaining 5 sts. Pull up tight and fasten securely.

Finger section

With rs facing, rejoin yarn B at base of thumb. Pick up and k3 sts previously cast on at base of thumb, then k all sts on left needle (42 sts).
Row 40 (ws): P all sts.
Rows 41–51: Beginning with a k row, work 11 rows in stockinette stitch, then break off yarn B.
Row 52: Using yarn C, p all sts. Break off yarn C.

Beaded top section

Thread 65 beads onto yarn A and work in pattern as follows.
Row 53 (rs): K2, (b1, k3) 4 times, b1, k to end.

New skills: adding beads

This simple technique allows you to add a sprinkling of beads to the surface of your mittens.

1 Thread a sewing needle that will easily pass through the beads with sewing thread. Knot the ends of the thread and pass the yarn through the loop made. Slide each bead onto the needle, then down the thread, and onto the yarn.

2 Work to the required position in the pattern and bring the yarn forward between the needles. Push a bead up the yarn until it is in front of the right needle.

3 Slip the next stitch knitwise, bring the bead up to sit in front of the slipped stitch, then take the yarn to the back of your work and continue the pattern.

Row 54 and all ws rows: P all sts.
Row 55: (K1, b1) 11 times, k to end.
Row 57: K4, (b1, k3) 4 times, b1, k to end.
Row 59: (K1, b1) 11 times, k to end.
Row 61: K2, (b1, k3) 4 times, b1, k to end.
Row 63: K2tog tbl, k1, (b1, k1) 8 times, k2tog, k2tog tbl, k to last 2 sts, k2tog (38 sts).
Row 65: K2tog tbl, k1, (b1, k3) 3 times, b1, k1, k2tog, k2tog tbl, k to last 2 sts, k2tog (34 sts).
Row 67: K2tog tbl, k1, (b1, k1) 6 times, k2tog, k2tog tbl, k to last 2 sts, k2tog (30 sts).
Row 69: K2tog tbl, k1, (b1, k3) twice, b1, k1, k2tog, k2tog tbl, k to last 2 sts, k2tog (26 sts).
Row 71: K2tog tbl, k1, (b1, k1) 4 times, k2tog, k2tog tbl, k to last 2 sts, k2tog (22 sts).

Break off yarn B, making sure you leave enough to sew the seam, and thread the yarn through remaining 5 sts. Pull up tight and fasten securely.

Finger section

With rs facing, rejoin yarn B at base of thumb. Pick up and k3 sts previously cast on at base of thumb, then k all sts on left needle (42 sts).

Row 40 (ws): P all sts.

Rows 41–51: Beginning with a k row, work 11 rows in stockinette stitch, then break off yarn B.

Row 52: Using yarn C, p to end. Break off yarn C.

Beaded top section

Thread 65 beads onto yarn A and work in pattern as follows.

Row 53 (rs): K23, (b1, k3) 4 times, b1, k2.

Row 54 and all ws rows: P all sts.

Row 55: K20, (b1, k1) 11 times.

Row 57: K21, (b1, k3) 5 times, k1.

Row 59: K20, (b1, k1) 11 times.

Row 61: K23, (b1, k3) 4 times, b1, k2.

Row 63: K2tog tbl, k17, k2tog, k2tog tbl, (k1, b1) 8 times, k1, k2tog (38 sts).

Row 65: K2tog tbl, k15, k2tog, k2tog tbl, k1, (b1, k3) 3 times, b1, k1, k2tog (34 sts).

Row 67: K2tog tbl, k13, k2tog, k2tog tbl, (k1, b1) 6 times, k1, k2tog (30 sts).

Row 69: K2tog tbl, k11, k2tog, k2tog tbl, k1, (b1, k3) twice, b1, k1, k2tog (26 sts).

Row 71: K2tog tbl, k9, k2tog, k2tog tbl, (k1, b1) 4 times, k1, k2tog (22 sts).

Row 72: P11, turn right needle so that both rs are facing, and use a third needle to bind off both sets of sts together knitwise.

Finishing

Weave in the ends and press gently, then sew the thumb and side seams using backstitch.

Row 72: P11, turn right needle so that both rs are facing, and use a third needle to bind off both sets of sts together knitwise.

LEFT MITTEN

Work first 22 rows as instructed for right mitten.

Shaping the thumb gusset

Row 23 (rs): K19, place marker on needle, m1, k1, m1, place marker on needle, k22 (44 sts).

Row 24 and all ws rows: P all sts.

Row 25: K all sts.

Row 27: K to marker, slip marker onto right needle, m1, k to next marker, m1, slip marker onto right needle, k to end (46 sts).

Row 29: K all sts.

Row 31: K to marker, slip marker onto right needle, m1, k to next marker, m1, slip marker onto right needle, k to end (48 sts).

Row 33: K all sts.

Row 35: K to marker, slip marker onto right needle, m1, k to next marker, m1, slip marker onto right needle, k to end (50 sts).

Row 37: K all sts.

Row 39: K29 and turn.

Knitting the thumb

Next row (ws): Cast on 3 sts, p these 3 sts, p11.

Next row (rs): Beginning with a k row, work 12 rows in stockinette stitch on these 14 sts only.

Shaping top of thumb

Next row (rs): K2, (k2tog, k1) 4 times (10 sts).

Next row: P all sts.

Next row: (K2tog) 5 times.

Knitted in shades of red and brown, these mittens are brightened with a decoration of bronze beads and orange stripes.

Project 3: Shaggy chenille wrap

This larger scale project is knitted in bulky merino/alpaca mix yarn. Although mainly worked in stockinette stitch, large bands of loop stitch in cotton chenille provide a contrast in texture. If preferred, the loops can be cut after knitting for a fringed effect.

before you start

Measurements
19½in (52cm) wide x 73¼in (186cm) long

Materials
Yarn A 6 x 4oz (100g) balls (approx. 109yds/100m per ball) bulky-weight merino/acrylic/alpaca mix yarn

Yarn B 3 x 4oz (100g) balls (approx. 152yds/140m per ball) bulky-weight cotton chenille yarn Use yarn B doubled throughout

Needles
1 pair size 11 (8mm) needles

Gauge
Yarn A—11 sts x 14 rows to 4in (10cm) measured over stockinette stitch using size 11 (8mm) needles

Abbreviations
k—knit; p—purl; rep—repeat; rs—right side; st(s)—stitch(es)

Knitting the wrap
Using size 11 (8mm) needles and yarn B doubled, cast on 57 sts. Break off yarn B and join yarn A.

First panel
Row 1 (rs): K10, *p1, k8, rep from * to last 2 sts, k2.
Row 2: K2, p to last 2 sts, k2.
Rows 3–34: Repeat rows 1 and 2 sixteen times.
Row 35: Without breaking off yarn A, join yarn B and use it to work this row in loop stitch.
Row 36: Using yarn B, k all sts, then break off yarn B.

Rows 37–40: Using yarn A, repeat rows 1 and 2 twice.
Rows 41–42: Repeat rows 35 and 36.

Remaining panels
Repeat pattern established by rows 1–42 of first panel to complete another five panels.
Repeat rows 1 and 2 seventeen times, ending with rs facing.
Break off yarn A and bind off knitwise using yarn B.

Finishing
Weave in the ends and steam gently on the wrong side.

New skills: loop stitch

The shaggy texture on this wrap is created using a special loop stitch. Remember to use the yarn doubled.

1 Knit 1 stitch, but do not slip it off the left needle. Bring the yarn to the front between the needles, pass the yarn clockwise around your left thumb to form a 2½in (6cm) loop, then take the yarn back between the needles. Knit into the stitch again, this time slipping it off the left needle.

2 Bring the yarn forward between the needles and wrap it over the right needle to make 1 stitch. Pass the 2 stitches just worked over this stitch. Pull the loop around your thumb to tighten it, then slip it off your thumb.

1

2

This big, cozy wrap is perfect for keeping out chilly weather. You could also adapt the pattern to knit a scarf-sized version by reducing the number of stitches and shortening the panels.

Project 4: Furry bag

This bag is so easy to make that you could knit it one evening and use it the next day. The bulky but lightweight yarn used to make the main body of the bag is a great contrast to the fur texture on the front panel. The handles are reinforced with petersham ribbon to prevent them from stretching, making this bag ideal for everyday use.

before you start

Measurements
12in (30cm) wide x 11½in (29cm) high

Materials
Yarn A 2 x 4oz (100g) balls (approx. 93yds/85m per ball) bulky-weight wool yarn

Yarn B 2 x 2oz (50g) balls (approx. 22yds/20m per ball) super bulky-weight mohair/wool mix fur-effect yarn

Two 12½in (32cm) x 1in (23mm) pieces petersham ribbon

Needles
1 pair size 13 (9mm) needles

Gauge
Yarn A—11 sts x 14 rows to 4in (10cm) measured over stockinette stitch using size 13 (9mm) needles

Abbreviations
k—knit; p—purl; rs—right side; st(s)—stitch(es); ws—wrong side

Knitting the bag
Using size 13 (9mm) needles and yarn A, cast on 33 sts.

Bag panel
Row 1 (rs): K1, (p1, k1) to end.
Row 2: P1, (k1, p1) to end.
Row 3: Beginning with a k row, continue in stockinette stitch until work measures 10in (25cm) from top of ribbing. End with ws facing for next row.
Next row (base fold line): K all sts.
Next row: Beginning with a k row, continue in stockinette stitch until work measures 10in (25cm) from base fold line.
Next row: Repeat rows 1 and 2. Bind off ribwise.

Fur panel
Using size 13 (9mm) needles and yarn B, cast on 24 sts.
Beginning with a p row, work in reverse stockinette stitch until panel measures 10in (25cm), ending with a ws row. Bind off knitwise.

Handles (make 2)
Using size 13 (9mm) needles and yarn A, cast on 43 sts.
Row 1: K1, (p1, k1) to end.
Row 2: P1, (k1, p1) to end.

Rows 3–7: Repeat rows 1 and 2 twice, then row 1 again. Bind off ribwise.

FINISHING
Bag
Weave in the ends on both pieces and press the bag panel carefully, folding it in half at the base fold line. Position the fur panel purl side up on one side of the bag panel, making sure that the cast-on edge is just on the base fold line and the bind-off edge is just below the ribbing. Overcast the fur panel in place using yarn B in order to disguise the join. With the fur panel on the inside, fold the bag panel along the base fold line so that the side edges and top ribbings align, then backstitch the side seams using yarn A.

Handles
Weave in the ends and fold each handle lengthwise so that the cast-on and bind-off edges match up, at the same time encasing a length of petersham ribbon. Overcast the two edges together using yarn A. Position each handle 2in (5cm) in from the side seams and 1in (2.5cm) below the ribbing. Using yarn A, attach each handle, taking care to sew through both handle and ribbon in order to hold them securely in place.

This funky fur bag works best in bold primary colors. If you can't find fur-effect yarn, knit the front panel in ordinary yarn using loop stitch instead (see page 44).

Project 5: Silky socks

These socks are sheer indulgence. There are two variations—one is knitted in pure silk yarn with beaded detail, the other in a cashmere/merino mix yarn with Swiss darned embroidery. You can use an ordinary pure wool or wool mix yarn if you are feeling less extravagant.

before you start

Measurements
One size to fit average-sized woman's feet

Materials
Beaded socks
2 x 2oz (50g) balls (approx. 201yds/186m per ball) sportweight silk yarn
52 small clear beads

Embroidered socks
3 x 1oz (25g) balls (approx. 137yds/125m per ball) sportweight cashmere/extra fine merino mix yarn
Scrap of yarn in a contrasting color for embroidery (leftover yarn from the beaded socks is used here)

Needles
1 pair size 2 (2.75mm) needles
1 pair size 3 (3.25mm) needles

Gauge
28 sts x 38 rows to 4in (10cm) measured over stockinette stitch using size 3 (3.25mm) needles

Abbreviations
b1—place 1 bead; k—knit; k2tog—knit 2 stitches together; p—purl; p2tog—purl 2 stitches together; rs—right side; st(s)—stitch(es); tbl—through back of loop; ws—wrong side

TIP: WORKING FROM CHARTS
The instructions for the top of these socks are given in both charted and written form, so they are a good project to try if working from charts is new to you because you can double-check what you are knitting from the chart against the written instructions if you are unsure of anything.

When knitting the beaded socks, take care to knit one sock from each chart for the left and right feet so that the beading will be on the outside of the ankle when worn. If knitting the embroidered socks, follow either chart because the embroidery is applied after knitting.

Chart instructions
For each beaded sock, thread 26 beads onto the yarn. Using size 2 (2.75mm) needles, cast on 58 sts. Work 6 rows in ribbing as indicated on the chart. Change to size 3 (3.25mm) needles and continue working from the chart, placing the beaded motif if appropriate and decreasing at the side seams where indicated. Decrease at the beginning of a purl row by p2tog tbl; decrease at the end of a purl row by p2tog. Decrease at the beginning of a knit row by k2tog tbl; decrease at the end of a knit row by k2tog. After working the final row of the chart, refer to the written instructions from shaping the heel onward. If you are making the embroidered socks, apply the Swiss darning when the knitting is complete.

Written instructions
RIGHT BEADED SOCK
Thread 26 beads onto the yarn. Using size 2 (2.75mm) needles, cast on 58 sts.
Row 1 (rs): (K1, p1) to end.
Row 2: (P1, k1) to end.
Rows 3–6: Repeat rows 1 and 2 twice.
Rows 7–16: Change to size 3 (3.25mm) needles and, beginning with a k row, work 10 rows in stockinette stitch.

Placing beaded motif
Row 17 (rs): K10, b1, k1, b1, k5, b1, k1, b1, k to end.
Row 18 and all ws rows: P all sts.
Row 19: K10, b1, k9, b1, k to end.
Row 21: K12, (b1, k1) 4 times, k to end.
Row 23: K11, (b1, k3) twice, b1, k to end.
Row 25: K12, b1, k5, b1, k to end.
Row 27: K13, b1, k3, b1, k to end.
Row 29: K2tog tbl, k12, b1, k1, b1, k to last 2 sts, k2tog (56 sts).
Row 31: K9, (b1, k4) twice, b1, k to end.
Row 33: K9, b1, k1, b1, k5, b1, k1, b1, k to end.
Rows 35–46: Beginning with a k row, work 12 rows in stockinette stitch.
Row 47: K2tog tbl, k to last 2 sts, k2tog (54 sts).
Row 48: P all sts.
Rows 49–56: Beginning with a k row, work another 8 rows in stockinette stitch.

Shaping the heel—first side
Row 57 (rs): K15 and turn.
Row 58 and all ws rows: P all sts.
Row 59: K14 and turn.
Row 61: K13 and turn.
Row 63: K12 and turn.

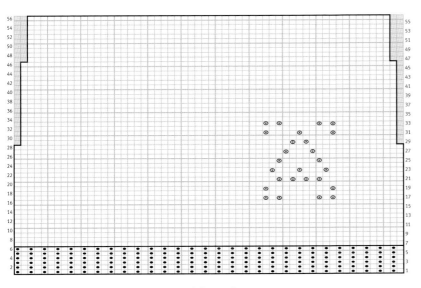

Right sock

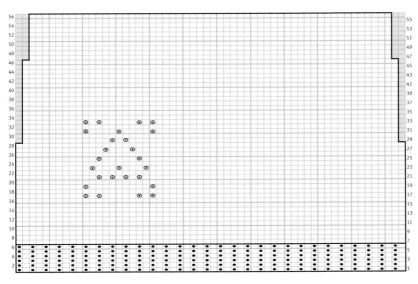

Left sock

KEY

☐	K on rs, p on ws
●	P on rs, k on ws
◉	B1
▨	Stitch not in work due to shaping

Row 65: K11 and turn.
Row 67: K10 and turn.
Row 69: K9 and turn.
Row 71: K8 and turn.
Row 73: K7 and turn.
Row 75: K8 and turn.
Row 77: K9 and turn.
Row 79: K10 and turn.
Row 81: K11 and turn.
Row 83: K12 and turn.
Row 85: K13 and turn.
Row 87: K14 and turn.
Row 89: K15 and turn.
Row 91: K all 54 sts.

Shaping the heel—second side

Row 92 (ws): P15 and turn.
Row 93 and all rs rows: K all sts.
Row 94: P14 and turn.
Row 96: P13 and turn.
Row 98: P12 and turn.
Row 100: P11 and turn.
Row 102: P10 and turn.
Row 104: P9 and turn.
Row 106: P8 and turn.
Row 108: P7 and turn.
Row 110: P8 and turn.
Row 112: P9 and turn.
Row 114: P10 and turn.
Row 116: P11 and turn.
Row 118: P12 and turn.
Row 120: P13 and turn.
Row 122: P14 and turn.
Row 124: P15 and turn.
Row 126: P all 54 sts, ending with
rs facing.

Knitting the foot

Rows 127–178: Beginning with a k row,
work 52 rows in stockinette stitch.

Shaping the toe

Row 179 (rs): K11, k2tog, k2, k2tog tbl,
k20, k2tog, k2, k2tog tbl, k11 (50 sts).
Row 180 and all ws rows: P all sts.
Row 181: K10, k2tog, k2, k2tog tbl, k18,
k2tog, k2, k2tog tbl, k10 (46 sts).
Row 183: K9, k2tog, k2, k2tog tbl, k16,
k2tog, k2, k2tog tbl, k9 (42 sts).

Pamper your feet with these luxurious silky and cashmere socks. You could easily adapt the heart motif into a design of your own to make them unique.

Row 185: K8, k2tog, k2, k2tog tbl, k14, k2tog, k2, k2tog tbl, k8 (38 sts).

Row 187: K7, k2tog, k2, k2tog tbl, k12, k2tog, k2, k2tog tbl, k7 (34 sts).

Row 189: K6, k2tog, k2, k2tog tbl, k10, k2tog, k2, k2tog tbl, k6 (30 sts).

Row 191: K5, k2tog, k2, k2tog tbl, k8, k2tog, k2, k2tog tbl, k5 (26 sts).

Row 193: K4, k2tog, k2, k2tog tbl, k6, k2tog, k2, k2tog tbl, k4 (22 sts).

Row 195: K3, k2tog, k2, k2tog tbl, k4, k2tog, k2, k2tog tbl, k3 (18 sts).

Row 196: P all sts. Bind off knitwise.

LEFT BEADED SOCK

Thread 26 beads onto the yarn. Using size 2 (2.75mm) needles, cast on 58 sts.

Row 1 (rs): (K1, p1) to end.

Row 2: (P1, k1) to end.

Rows 3–6: Repeat rows 1 and 2 twice.

Rows 7–16: Change to size 3 (3.25mm) needles and, beginning with a k row, work 10 rows in stockinette stitch.

Placing beaded motif

Row 17 (rs): K37, b1, k1, b1, k5, b1, k1, b1, k to end.

Row 18 and all ws rows: P all sts.

Row 19: K37, b1, k9, b1, k to end.

Row 21: K39, (b1, k1) 4 times, k to end.

Row 23: K38, (b1, k3) twice, b1, k to end.

Row 25: K39, b1, k5, b1, k to end.

Row 27: K40, b1, k3, b1, k to end.

Row 29: K2tog tbl, k40, b1, k1, b1, k to last 2 sts, k2tog (56 sts).

Row 31: K36, (b1, k4) twice, b1, k to end.

Row 33: K36, b1, k1, b1, k5, b1, k1, b1, k to end.

Rows 35–196: Follow instructions for right sock from row 35 to end.

Finishing

Weave in the ends and gently press on the wrong side. Sew the center back seam very neatly with backstitch.

EMBROIDERED SOCKS (MAKE 2)

Using size 2 (2.75mm) needles, cast on 58 sts.

Row 1 (rs): (K1, p1) to end.

Row 2: (P1, k1) to end.

Rows 3–6: Repeat rows 1 and 2 twice.

Rows 7–28: Change to size 3 (3.25mm) needles and, beginning with a k row, work 22 rows in stockinette stitch.

Row 29 (rs): K2tog tbl, k to last 2 sts, k2tog (56 sts).

Row 30: P all sts.

Rows 31–46: Beginning with a k row, work another 16 rows in stockinette stitch.

Row 47 (rs): K2tog tbl, k to last 2 sts, k2tog (54 sts).

Row 48: P all sts.

Rows 49–56: Beginning with a k row, work another 8 rows in stockinette stitch, ending with rs facing for start of heel shaping.

Rows 57–196: Follow the written instructions for the beaded sock from shaping the heel onward.

Finishing

Weave in the ends. Using contrast yarn, Swiss darn the motif, placing each embroidery stitch in the same places as the beads indicated on the chart on page 49. The motif should be 10 sts in from the side edge and 10 rows below the last row of ribbing. Remember to place the embroidery on opposite sides for the left and right socks. Gently press on the wrong side and sew the center back seam very neatly with backstitch.

Project 6: Cozy cashmere hat

The bulky cashmere/merino mix yarn used for this hat makes it beautifully cozy to wear. Fully fashioned shaping creates the squared crown, round sides, and cupped earflaps, while purl stitches are worked to produce the subtle patterned stripe.

before you start

Measurements
One size to fit average-sized woman's head

Materials
3 x 1oz (25g) balls (approx. 51yds/43m per ball) bulky-weight cashmere/merino mix yarn

Needles
1 pair size 11 (8mm) needles

Gauge
12 sts x 19 rows to 4in (10cm) measured over stockinette stitch using size 11 (8mm) needles

Abbreviations
beg—beginning; k—knit; k2tog—knit 2 stitches together; m1—make 1 stitch by picking up horizontal bar before next stitch, putting it onto left needle, then purling into back of it; p—purl; p2tog—purl 2 stitches together; rem—remaining; rep—repeat; rs—right side; st(s)—stitch(es); tbl—through back of loop

Knitting the hat
Using size 11 (8mm) needles, cast on 52 sts.
Row 1 (rs): (K1, p1) to end.
Row 2: (P11, k1, p2, k1, p11) twice.
Row 3: (K9, p1, k2tog, k2, k2tog tbl, p1, k9) twice (48 sts).
Row 4: (P9, k1, p4, k1, p9) 4 times.
Row 5: (K8, p1, k2tog, k2, k2tog tbl, p1, k8) twice (44 sts).
Row 6: (P8, k1, p4, k1, p8) 4 times.
Row 7: (K8, p1, k4, p1, k8) twice.
Row 8: (P8, k1, p4, k1, p8) twice.
Row 9: (K9, m1, k4, m1, k9) twice (48 sts).
Row 10: (P9, k1, p4, k1, p9) twice.
Row 11: (K2, m1, k8, m1, k2) 4 times (56 sts).
Row 12: (P2, k1, p8, k1, p2) 4 times.
Row 13: (K2, m1, k10, m1, k2) 4 times (64 sts).
Row 14: (P2, k1, p10, k1, p2) 4 times.
Row 15: (K2, m1, k12, m1, k2) 4 times (72 sts).
Row 16: (P2, k1, p12, k1, p2) 4 times.

Texture pattern
Row 17 (rs): K1, *p1, k2, rep from * to last 2 sts, p1, k1.
Row 18: K1, *p4, k2, rep from * to last 5 sts, p4, k1.
Row 19: P1, *k4, p2, rep from * to last 5 sts, k4, p1.
Row 20: P1, *k1, p2, rep from * to last 2 sts, k1, p1.
Row 21: K2, *p2, k4, rep from * to last 4 sts, p2, k2.
Row 22: P2, *k2, p4, rep from * to last 4 sts, k2, p2.
Row 23: P2tog, *k2, p4, (k2, p1) twice, rep from * to last 10 sts, k2, p4, k2, p2tog tbl (70 sts).
Row 24: *P3, k4, p3, k2, rep from * to last 10 sts, p3, k4, p3.
Row 25: *K3, p4, k3, p2, rep from * to last 10 sts, k3, p4, k3.
Row 26: P3, *k4, (p2, k1) twice, p2, rep from * to last 7 sts, k4, p3.
Row 27: P2tog, p1, *k4, p2, rep from * to last 7 sts, k4, p1, p2tog tbl (68 sts).
Row 28: *K2, p4, rep from * to last 2 sts, k2.
Row 29: *K2, p1, rep from * to last 2 sts, k2.
Row 30: P3, *k2, p4, rep from * to last 5 sts, k2, p3.
Row 31: K3, *p2, k4, rep from * to last 5 sts, p2, k3.
Row 32: *P2, k1, rep from * to last 2 sts, p2.
Row 33: *P2, k4, rep from * to last 2 sts, p2.
Row 34: *K2, p4, rep from * to last 2 sts, k2.
Row 35: K2, *p4, (k2, p1) twice, k2, rep from * to last 6 sts, p4, k2.
Row 36: P2tog, *k4, p3, k2, p3, rep from * to last 6 sts, k4, p2tog (66 sts).
Row 37: K1, *p4, k3, p2, k3, rep from * to last 5 sts, p4, k1.
Row 38: P1, *k4, (p2, k1) twice, p2, rep from * to last 5 sts, k4, p1.

First earflap
Break off yarn and slip first 24 sts onto a stitch holder. Rejoin yarn to rem sts and bind off next 18 sts knitwise. Complete the row as follows.
Row 39 (rs): K2, p1, k to last 4 sts, p1,

k2tog, k1 (23 sts).

Row 40: P2, k1, p to last 3 sts, p2tog tbl, p1 (22 sts).

Row 41: K to last 3 sts, p1, k2.

Row 42: Bind off 6 sts at beg of row purlwise, p to end (16 sts).

Row 43: K all sts.

Row 44: P all sts.

Rows 45–46: Repeat rows 43 and 44.

Row 47: K6, k2tog tbl, k2tog, k6 (14 sts).

Row 48: P all sts.

Row 49: K5, k2tog tbl, k2tog, k5 (12 sts).

Row 50: P all sts.

Row 51: K4, k2tog tbl, k2tog, k4 (10 sts).

Row 52: P2tog, p to last 2 sts, p2tog tbl (8 sts).

Row 53: (K2tog tbl) twice, (k2tog) twice (4 sts). Bind off purlwise.

Second earflap

With rs facing, slip sts from holder back onto needle and rejoin yarn.

Next row (rs): K1, k2tog tbl, p1, k to end (23 sts).

Next row: P1, p2tog, p to last 3 sts, k1, p2 (22 sts).

Next row: Bind off 6 sts at beg of row knitwise, k to end (16 sts).

Next row: P all sts.

Continue as for first earflap from row 43 to end.

Finishing

Weave in the ends and steam gently on the wrong side. Fold in half with right sides facing and backstitch the back seam very neatly. Turn the hat right side out and fold it so that the seam is at the center back of the hat. Overcast the top edges together.

With its pointed corners and cupped earflaps, this hat is cute to look at and warm to wear.

Project 7: Beaded pompon scarf

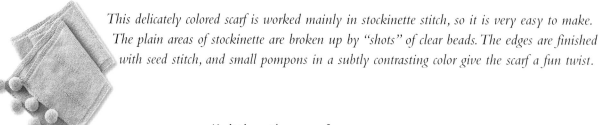

This delicately colored scarf is worked mainly in stockinette stitch, so it is very easy to make. The plain areas of stockinette are broken up by "shots" of clear beads. The edges are finished with seed stitch, and small pompons in a subtly contrasting color give the scarf a fun twist.

before you start

Measurements
8¼in (21cm) wide x 56¾in (144cm) long excluding pompon edge

Materials
2oz (50g) balls (approx. 200yds/183m per ball) sportweight merino yarn in 2 colors:
Yarn A   Pale blue x 3 balls
Yarn B   Pale green x 1 ball
540 small clear beads

Needles
1 pair size 3 (3.25mm) needles

Gauge
28 sts x 36 rows to 4in (10cm) measured over stockinette stitch using size 3 (3.25mm) needles

Abbreviations
b1—place 1 bead; k—knit; p—purl; patt—pattern; rs—right side; st(s)—stitch(es); ws—wrong side

Knitting the scarf
Thread 180 beads onto each of the three balls of yarn A. Using size 3 (3.25mm) needles and yarn B, cast on 60 sts. Break off yarn B and join yarn A.
Row 1 (rs): (K1, p1) to end.
Row 2: Repeat row 1.

Starting beaded pattern
Row 3: (K1, p1) twice, k to last 5 sts, (p1, k1) twice, p1.
Row 4: (P1, k1) twice, p to last 5 sts, (k1, p1) twice, k1.
Rows 5–20: Repeat rows 3 and 4 eight times.
Row 21: (K1, p1) twice, k2, (b1, k1) 16 times, k17, (p1, k1) twice, p1.
Row 22: Repeat row 4.
Row 23: (K1, p1) twice, (k1, b1) 15 times, k21, (p1, k1) twice, p1.
Row 24: Repeat row 4.
Rows 25–42: Repeat rows 3 and 4 nine times.
Row 43: (K1, p1) twice, k34, (b1, k1) 8 times, (k1, p1) to end.
Row 44: Repeat row 4.
Row 45: (K1, p1) twice, k25, (b1, k1) 13 times, (p1, k1) twice, p1.
Row 46: Repeat row 4.
Rows 47–64: Repeat rows 3 and 4 nine times.
Row 65: (K1, p1) twice, k8, (b1, k1) 11 times, k21, (p1, k1) twice, p1.
Row 66: Repeat row 4.
Row 67: (K1, p1) twice, k13, (b1, k1) 7 times, k24, (p1, k1) twice, p1.
Row 68: Repeat row 4.

Rows 69–86: Repeat rows 3 and 4 nine times.
Row 87: (K1, p1) twice, k32, (b1, k1) 9 times, (k1, p1) to end.
Row 88: Repeat row 4.
Row 89: (K1, p1) twice, k23, (b1, k1) 11 times, k6, (p1, k1) twice, p1.
Row 90: Repeat row 4.

Completing beaded pattern
Continue to work in patt as established by rows 3–90 until five repeats have been completed.
Repeat rows 3 and 4 nine times.
Next row (rs): (K1, p1) to end.
Next row (ws): Repeat previous row. Break off yarn A, then bind off knitwise using yarn B.

Finishing
Weave in the ends and steam gently on the wrong side. Using yarn A, make eight 1¼in (3cm) diameter pompons, leaving the ends of yarn that you use to tie the pompons about 6in (15cm) long. Use these to attach four pompons to the cast-on edge, one at each corner and the other two spaced evenly between, and four to the opposite end of the scarf.

New skills

Adding beads, see page 41
Making pompons, see page 98

The delicate colors of this scarf work well with all hair and skin colors, or you could use strong, vibrant shades to make a funkier version.

Project 8: Classic-style gloves

This classic style of glove is given a modern twist by the use of a bright color contrast on the cast-on edge and an irregular ribbing detail at the cuff. This pair has been knitted in bright pink with an orange trim, but a more subtle color combination would work equally well.

before you start

Measurements

One size to fit average-sized woman's hands

Materials

2 x 2oz (50g) balls (approx. 200yds/183m per ball) sportweight merino yarn
Scrap of same yarn in a contrasting color

Needles

1 pair size 2 (2.75mm) needles

Gauge

30 sts x 42 rows to 4in (10cm) measured over stockinette stitch using size 2 (2.75mm) needles

Abbreviations

beg—beginning; k—knit; m1—make 1 stitch by picking up horizontal bar before next stitch, putting it onto left needle, then knitting into back of it; p—purl; rem—remaining; rep—repeat; rs—right side; st(s)—stitch(es); ws—wrong side

Knitting the gloves (make 2)

Using size 2 (2.75mm) needles and contrast yarn, cast on 58 sts.
Row 1 (rs): P2, (k2, p2) to end.
Row 2: K2, (p2, k2) to end. Break off contrast yarn.
Rows 3–8: Join main yarn and repeat rows 1 and 2 three times.
Row 9: P2, *k6, (p2, k2) twice, p2, rep from * to last 8 sts, k6, p2.
Row 10: K2, *p6, (k2, p2) twice, k2, rep from * to last 8 sts, p6, k2.
Rows 11–14: Repeat rows 9 and 10 twice.
Row 15: P1, k11, (p2, k14) twice, p2, k11, p1.
Row 16: K1, p11, (k2, p14) twice, k2, p11, k1.
Rows 17–30: Repeat rows 15 and 16 seven times.
Rows 31–38: Beginning with a k row, work 8 rows in stockinette stitch.

Shaping the thumb gusset

Row 39 (rs): K27, m1, k4, m1, k27 (60 sts).
Row 40 and all ws rows: P all sts.
Row 41: K27, m1, k6, m1, k27 (62 sts).
Row 43: K27, m1, k8, m1, k27 (64 sts).
Row 45: K27, m1, k10, m1, k27 (66 sts).
Row 47: K27, m1, k12, m1, k27 (68 sts).
Row 49: K27, m1, k14, turn.

Knitting the thumb

Next row (ws): Cast on 1 st, p this st, p15, turn (16 sts).
Next row: Cast on 2 sts, k these 2 sts, k16 (18 sts).
Beginning with a p row, work another 25 rows in stockinette stitch on these 18 sts only, ending with rs facing.
Break off yarn, making sure you leave enough to sew the seam, and thread the yarn through the sts. Pull up tight and fasten securely. Sew the thumb seam using backstitch.

Finger section

With rs facing, rejoin yarn to rem sts. Pick up and k2 sts previously cast on at base of thumb, then k to end (56 sts).
Row 50 (ws): P all sts.
Rows 51–68: Beginning with a p row, work 18 rows in stockinette stitch.
Row 69 (rs): K36 and turn.

Shaping first finger

Next row (ws): Cast on 1 st, p this stitch, p16, turn (17 sts).
Next row: Cast on 1 st, k this stitch, k17 (18 sts).
Beginning with a p row, work another 27 rows in stockinette stitch on these 18 sts only, ending with rs facing.
Break off yarn, making sure you leave enough to sew the seam, and thread the yarn through the sts. Pull up tight and fasten securely. Backstitch the finger seam.

Shaping second finger

Next row (rs): Rejoin yarn to rem sts. Pick up and k2 sts previously cast on at base of first finger, k7, turn.
Next row: Cast on 1 st, p this stitch, p16, turn (17 sts).
Next row: Cast on 1 st, k this stitch, k17, turn (18 sts).

The classic design of these gloves makes them very versatile to wear. Make a design statement with your choice of color.

Beginning with a p row, work another 31 rows in stockinette stitch on these 18 sts only, ending with rs facing. Finish off as for first finger.

Shaping third finger

Next row (rs): Rejoin yarn to rem sts. Pick up and k2 sts previously cast on at base of second finger, k7, turn.

Next row: Cast on 1 st, p this stitch, p16, turn (17 sts).

Next row: Cast on 1 st, k this stitch, k17, turn (18 sts).

Beginning with a p row, work another 27 rows in stockinette stitch on these 18 sts only, ending with rs facing. Finish off as for first finger.

Shaping fourth finger

Next row (rs): Rejoin yarn to rem sts. Pick up and k2 sts previously cast on at base of third finger, k to end, turn.

Next row: Beginning with a p row, work another 21 rows in stockinette stitch on these 14 sts only. Break off yarn, leaving an end about 8–12in (20–30cm) long. Thread the yarn through the sts. Pull up tight and fasten securely. Backstitch the finger/side seam.

Finishing

Weave in the ends and press the gloves (do not press the ribbing).

The irregular ribbing and contrasting colored trim around the wrist provide a pretty decorative detail.

Project 9: Legwarmers

Funky, chunky, and quick to knit, these legwarmers are worked in an irregular brioche ribbing texture that is achieved by knitting into the stitch one row below. The cast-on and bind-off edges are knitted in a contrasting color, although the legwarmers can be completed in a single color if preferred.

before you start

Measurements

One size to fit average-sized woman's legs

Materials

2oz (50g) balls (approx. 95yds/87m per ball) Aran-weight extra fine merino yarn in 2 colors:

Yarn A   Green x 3 balls

Yarn B   Brown x 1 ball

Needles

1 pair size 7 (4.5mm) needles

Gauge

21 sts x 27 rows to 4in (10cm) measured over reverse stockinette stitch using size 7 (4.5mm) needles

Abbreviations

k—knit; k1b—work next stitch by inserting needle into stitch on row below and knit it together with stitch above; p—purl; rs—right side; st(s)—stitch(es)

Knitting the legwarmers (make 2)

Using size 7 (4.5mm) needles and yarn B, cast on 59 sts.

Row 1 (rs): P4, (k1, p4) to end.

Row 2: K4, (p1, k4) to end.

Row 3: P4, (k1b, p4) to end.

Row 4: Repeat row 2.

Break off yarn B and join yarn A.

Rows 5–10: Repeat rows 3 and 4 three times.

Irregular ribbing pattern

Row 11: P4, k1b, p9, (k1b, p4) 7 times, k1b, p to end.

Row 12: K9, (p1, k4) 7 times, p1, k9, p1, k to end.

Rows 13–14: Repeat rows 11 and 12.

Row 15: P4, k1b, p9, (k1b, p4) 3 times, k1b, p9, (k1b, p4) twice, k1b, p to end.

Row 16: K9, (p1, k4) twice, p1, k9, (p1, k4) 3 times, p1, k9, p1, k to end.

Row 17: P4, k1b, p14, (k1b, p4) twice, k1b, p9, (k1b, p4) twice, k1b, p to end.

Row 18: K9, (p1, k4) twice, p1, k9, (p1, k4) twice, p1, k14, p1, k to end.

Row 19: P4, k1b, p14, (k1b, p4) twice, k1b, p9, k1b, p4, k1b, p to end.

Row 20: K14, p1, k4, p1, k9, p1, (k4, p1) twice, k14, p1, k to end.

Rows 21–22: Repeat rows 19 and 20.

Row 23: P4, k1b, p14, k1b, (p9, k1b) twice, p4, k1b, p to end.

Row 24: K14, p1, k4, p1, (k9, p1) twice, k14, p1, k to end.

Rows 25–26: Repeat rows 23 and 24.

Row 27: P4, k1b, p14, k1b, (p9, k1b) twice, p4, k1b, p4, k1, p to end.

Row 28: K9, p1, (k4, p1) twice, (k9, p1) twice, k14, p1, k to end.

Row 29: P4, k1b, p14, k1b, (p9, k1b) twice, (p4, k1b) twice, p to end.

Row 30: K9, p1, (k4, p1) twice, (k9, p1) twice, k14, p1, k to end.

Row 31: P4, k1b, p14, k1b, p9, k1b, p14, k1b, p4, k1b, p to end.

Row 32: K9, p1, k4, p1, k14, p1, k9, p1, k14, p1, k to end.

Rows 33–36: Repeat rows 31 and 32 twice.

Row 37: P4, k1b, p4, k1, p9, k1b, p24, k1b, p4, k1b, p to end.

Row 38: K9, p1, k4, p1, k24, p1, k9, p1, k4, p1, k to end.

Row 39: (P4, k1b) twice, p9, k1b, p24, k1b, p4, k1b, p to end.

Row 40: Repeat row 38.

Row 41: (P9, k1b) twice, p24, k1b, p4, k1b, p to end.

Row 42: K9, p1, k4, p1, k24, p1, k9, p1, k to end.

Row 43: (P9, k1b) twice, p19, k1, (p4, k1b) twice, p to end.

Row 44: K9, p1, (k4, p1) twice, k19, p1, k9, p1, k to end.

Row 45: (P9, k1b) twice, p19, k1b, (p4, k1b) twice, p to end.

Row 46: Repeat row 44.

Row 47: (P9, k1b) twice, p19, k1b, p9, k1b, p4, k1, p to end.

Row 48: (K4, p1) twice, k9, p1, k19, p1, k9, p1, k to end.

Row 49: (P9, k1b) twice, p19, k1b, p9, k1b, p4, k1b, p to end.

Row 50: Repeat row 48.

Row 51: P4, k1, p4, k1b, p9, k1b, p9, k1, (p9, k1b) twice, p4, k1b, p to end.

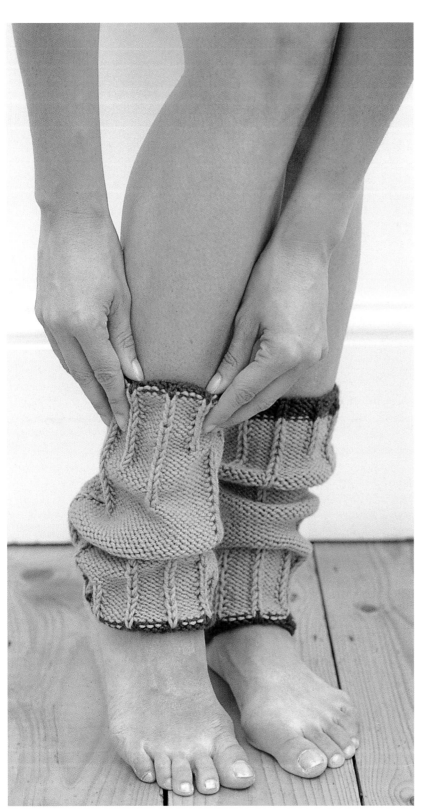

Row 52: (K4, p1) twice, (k9, p1) 4 times, k4, p1, k to end.

Row 53: (P4, k1b) twice, (p9, k1b) 4 times, p4, k1b, p to end.

Rows 54–55: Repeat rows 52 and 53.

Row 56: Repeat row 52.

Row 57: (P4, k1b) twice, (p9, k1b) twice, p4, k1, p4, k1b, p9, k1b, p4, k1b, p to end.

Row 58: (K4, p1) twice, k9, p1, (k4, p1) twice, (k9, p1) twice, k4, p1, k to end.

Row 59: (P4, k1b) twice, (p9, k1b) twice, (p4, k1b) twice, p9, k1b, p4, k1b, p to end.

Row 60: Repeat row 58.

Row 61: (P4, k1b) twice, p4, k1, p4, k1b, p9, k1b, (p4, k1b) twice, p9, k1b, p4, k1b, p to end.

Row 62: (K4, p1) twice, k9, p1, (k4, p1) twice, k9, p1, (k4, p1) 3 times, k to end.

Row 63: (P4, k1b) 3 times, p9, k1, (p4, k1b) 3 times, p9, k1b, p4, k1b, p to end.

Row 64: (K4, p1) twice, k9, p1, (k4, p1) 3 times, k9, p1, (k4, p1) twice, k to end.

Row 65: (P4, k1b) 3 times, p9, (k1b, p4) 3 times, k1b, p9, k1b, p4, k1b, p to end.

Row 66: Repeat row 64.

Row 67: (P4, k1b) 3 times, p9, (k1b, p4) 4 times, k1, (p4, k1b) twice, p to end.

Row 68: (K4, p1) 7 times, k9, p1, (k4, p1) twice, k to end.

Row 69: (P4, k1b) 3 times, p9, (k1b, p4) to end.

Row 70: Repeat row 68.

Row 71: (P4, k1b) 3 times, p4, k1, p4, (k1b, p4) to end.

Row 72: K4, (p1, k4) to end.

Row 73: P4, (k1b, p4) to end.

Rows 74–77: Repeat rows 72 and 73 twice.

Row 78: Repeat row 72. Break off yarn A.

Final contrast edge

Row 79: Join yarn B and repeat row 73.

Row 80: Repeat row 72. Bind off knitwise.

Finishing

Weave in the ends and sew the back seam using backstitch. Do not press.

Wear the legwarmers any way you want—scrunched around your ankles or fitted over your calves. Both ways look good.

Project 10: Patchwork bag

The front of this patchwork bag consists of three vertical strips blanket stitched together, while the back is made up of a single panel of stockinette stitch knitted with horizontal stripes of color. The pieces are sewn together and then felted in the washing machine, making the bag beautifully soft and simple.

before you start

Measurements	11in (28cm) wide x 12½in (32cm) high after felting
Materials	2oz (50g) balls (approx. 123yds/113m per ball) DK tweed-effect wool yarn in 6 colors:

Yarn A	Red x 1 ball	**Yarn B**	Purple x 1 ball
Yarn C	Pink x 1 ball	**Yarn D**	Yellow x 1 ball
Yarn E	Green x 1 ball	**Yarn F**	Blue x 1 ball

52 large blue beads

Needles	1 pair size 9 (5.5mm) needles
Gauge	**After felting**—18 sts x 30 rows to 4in (10cm) measured over stockinette stitch using size 9 (5.5mm) needles
Abbreviations	b1—place 1 bead; k—knit; p—purl; rs—right side; sl—slip stitch from left to right needle without working it; st(s)—stitch(es); ws—wrong side

Knitting the bag

Front strips

The three pieces that make up the front panel of the bag are shown on the charts on pages 64–65. Using size 9 (5.5mm) needles in each case, cast on 19 sts in the yarn that appears on line 1 of the chart. When the last row of the chart has been completed, and still using the same yarn, work 4 rows in garter stitch and bind off knitwise.

Back panel

Using size 9 (5.5mm) needles and yarn A, cast on 58 sts.

Rows 1–32: Beginning with a k row, work 32 rows in stockinette stitch.

Rows 33–64: Change to yarn D and work another 32 rows in stockinette stitch.

TIP: SUCCESSFUL FELTING

Successful felting using a washing machine is about trial and error. This is largely due to differences in makes of machine and wash program. Too cold a wash for too short a time and the fabric will not shrink enough; too hot a wash for too long and your knitting could resemble concrete. It is therefore a good idea to knit a test swatch for this project—20 sts x 32 rows on size 9 (5.5mm) needles. Wash the piece at 100°F (40°C) on your machine's quick or half-wash program (approx. 30–40 minutes long) using about ½ cup of a detergent suitable for wool use. Putting a towel into the wash will contribute to the felting process. When the wash cycle is complete, let the piece dry and then measure your swatch. The extra stitches and rows should allow for the fabric rolling during the felting process. If your 18 sts x 30 rows are smaller than 4in (10cm), the piece has felted too much, so shorten the wash cycle. If larger, wash for a bit longer. It is important that you keep notes of all details while you experiment.

You could make this patchwork bag from leftover balls of yarn from other projects. Just make sure that the weight and gauge of the yarns are the same.

Rows 65–96: Change to yarn C and work another 32 rows in stockinette stitch.

Rows 97–100: Change to yarn F and k the next 4 rows. Bind off knitwise.

Handles (make 2)

Measure six 10ft (3m) lengths of yarns B, D, and F. Knot them together at one end and braid them until you are 2in (5cm) from the other end. Tie another knot.

FINISHING
Bag

Weave in the ends on each of the three front pieces. Place strips 1 and 2 together, wrong sides facing. Match up the squares and edges, then sew the seam on the right side using blanket stitch. Join the remaining piece in the same way. Place the front and back panels right sides facing, taking care to match the edges, and backstitch the pieces together. Felt the completed bag and braided handles and allow to dry. Press the bag gently on the wrong side.

Handles

Cut four 17¼in (44cm) long handles from the felted braid. Position one handle 2¾in (7cm) in from the side seams and 1½in (4cm) below the top edge of the bag. Pin it in place. Pin another handle next to it (toward the side seam). Sew the handles in place on the inside, using colors that will not show.

New skills

Adding beads, see page 41

KEY

- Yarn A—Red
- Yarn B—Purple
- Yarn C—Pink
- Yarn D—Yellow
- Yarn E—Green
- Yarn F—Blue
- K on rs, p on ws
- P on rs, k on ws
- Sl st knitwise on rs, purlwise on ws
- B1

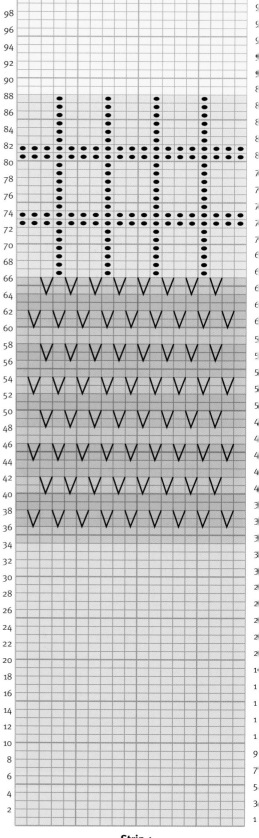

Strip 1

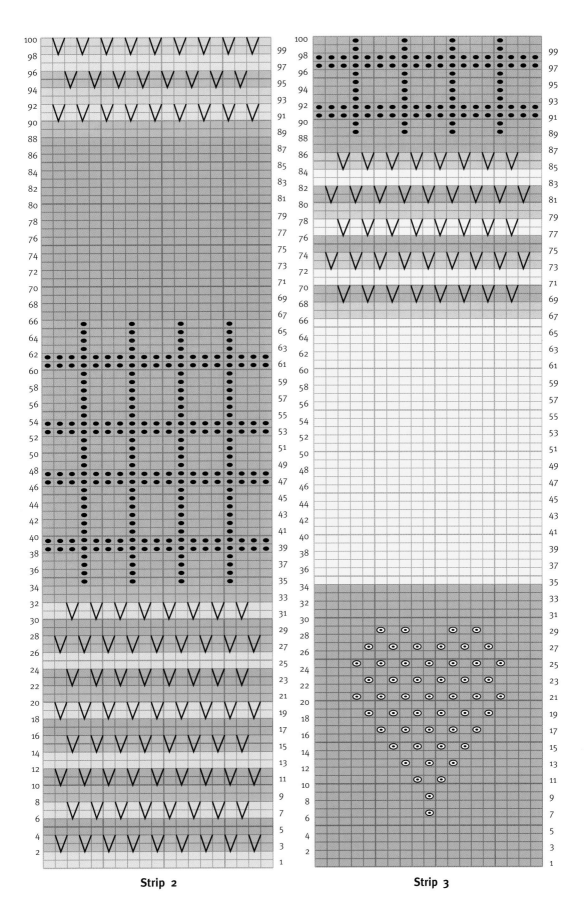

Strip 2   **Strip 3**

Project 11: Lacy beaded scarf

This scarf combines lace and colored beading for a very feminine look and is finished with beaded fringing. Although lace work can look difficult, full chart instructions make it easier to place the pattern and keep track of your knitting progress.

before you start

Measurements

8¾in (22cm) wide x 40in (102cm) long excluding fringing

Materials

4 x 2oz (50g) balls (approx. 123yds/113m per ball) DK merino/cotton mix yarn
256 large clear beads
228 large white beads
204 large mauve beads

Needles

1 pair size 5 (3.75mm) needles

Gauge

24 sts x 30 rows to 4in (10cm) measured over stockinette stitch using size 5 (3.75mm) needles

Abbreviations

k—knit; k2tog—knit 2 stitches together; p—purl; rs—right side; skpo—slip 1 stitch knitwise from left to right needle without working it, knit 1 stitch, pass slipped stitch over knitted stitch; st(s)—stitch(es); ws—wrong side; yf—bring yarn forward between needles

New skills

Adding beads, see page 41

Knitting the scarf

Thread each ball of yarn with beads in the correct color sequence (see page 68). Using size 5 (3.75mm) needles, cast on 59 sts. Work in lace and bead pattern as indicated on the chart on page 68 until you have completed 4 repeats, using a new ball of beaded yarn for each repeat and ending with a wrong side row. Repeat rows 1 and 2, then bind off knitwise.

New skills:
attaching fringing

For each piece of fringing, thread 2 beads onto one end and secure with a knot about 1in (2cm) from the end; repeat at the other end with another 2 beads. You can bead the fringing in a random or regular color sequence.

1 Insert a crochet hook from the front of the work into the first lace hole.

2 Fold a length of beaded yarn in half and pull it through to the front of the work until the loop of yarn is about 1in (2.5cm) long.

3 Pull the beaded ends of the yarn through the loop and tighten the knot. Continue inserting a piece of beaded fringing into each lace hole along both ends of the scarf.

Finishing

Weave in the ends and press the scarf on the wrong side. Cut ninety 5½in (14cm) lengths of yarn for the fringing (45 for each end of the scarf). Bead the fringing and attach it to the scarf.

If you wish to knit the scarf in a different color yarn, try to find a combination of bead colors in similar tones to complement it.

KEY

☐ K on rs, p on ws
◉ P on rs, k on ws
◿ K2tog
○ Yf
◉ Place 1 mauve bead
◉ Place 1 clear bead
• Place 1 white bead
◺ Skpo

TIP: BEADING SEQUENCE

When knitting with beads of more than one color, you need to thread them onto the yarn in the opposite order to which they will be worked into the knitting before casting on. Following the chart, start at the top and read down from left to right on each of the beading rows.

The beading sequence for this project is: 3 clear, 1 mauve, 1 clear, 2 mauve, 1 clear, 9 mauve, 2 white, 1 mauve, 2 white, 2 clear, 2 white, 1 mauve, 12 white, 14 clear, 1 mauve, 1 clear, 1 mauve, 2 clear, 4 mauve, 2 clear, 2 white, 1 mauve, 2 white, 2 clear, 4 white, 2 clear, 1 white, 24 clear

The intricate lace and
bead work of this scarf
are complemented
perfectly by the long
beaded fringing.

Project 12: Chunky ruffle beanie

This beanie knitted in bulky-weight yarn has a ruffle detail at the top of the crown and vertical lace holes in each panel. Although the hat has been worked in two colors, it would look equally good knitted in a single color.

before you start

Measurements
One size to fit average-sized woman's head

Materials
2oz (50g) balls (approx. 42yds/38m per ball) super bulky-weight wool/acrylic mix yarn in 2 colors:

Yarn A   Red x 2 balls

Yarn B   Bracken x 1 ball

Needles
1 pair size 13 (9mm) needles

Gauge
11 sts x 15 rows to 4in (10cm) measured over stockinette stitch using size 13 (9mm) needles

Abbreviations
inc 1—increase 1 stitch by knitting into front and back of next stitch; k—knit; k2tog—knit 2 stitches together; p—purl; rep—repeat; rs—right side; st(s)—stitch(es); ws—wrong side; yf—bring yarn forward between needles

Knitting the hat
Using size 13 (9mm) needles and yarn A, cast on 56 sts.

Row 1 (rs): (P1, k1) to end.

Row 2: (P1, k1) to end.

Using the intarsia technique to change colors (see page 32), work the hat in vertical striped panels as follows.

Row 3: K15 with yarn A, join yarn B, and k13 with yarn B. Join a new supply of yarn A and k15. Join a new supply of yarn B and k13.

Row 4: P13 with yarn B, p15 with yarn A, p13 with yarn B, p15 with yarn A.

Row 5: *Using yarn A, k7, yf, k2tog, k6. Using yarn B, k6, yf, k2tog, k5. Rep from * to end.

Row 6: P all sts, keeping color panels correct.

Row 7: K all sts, keeping color panels correct.

Row 8: P all sts, keeping color panels correct.

Rows 9–20: Repeat rows 5–8 three times.

Shaping the crown
Row 21: *Using yarn A, k2tog, k5, yf, k2tog, k4, k2tog. Using yarn B, k2tog, k4, yf, k2tog, k3, k2tog. Rep from * to end.

Row 22 and all ws rows: P to end, keeping color panels correct.

Row 23: *Using yarn A, k2tog, k9, k2tog. Using yarn B, k2tog, k7, k2tog. Rep from * to end.

Row 25: *Using yarn A, k2tog, k3, yf, k2tog, k2, k2tog. Using yarn B, k2tog, k2, yf, k2tog, k1, k2tog. Rep from * to end.

Row 27: *Using yarn A, k2tog, k5, k2tog. Using yarn B, k2tog, k3, k2tog. Rep from * to end.

Row 29: *Using yarn A, k2tog, k3, k2tog. Using yarn B, k2tog, k1, k2tog. Rep from * to end.

Row 30: P all sts, keeping color panels correct.

Break off both ends of yarn B.

Making the ruffle
Use yarn A only.

Row 31 (rs): (K1, yf, k2tog) 5 times, k1 (16 sts).

Row 32: P all sts.

Row 33: *K1, inc 1, rep from * to end (24 sts).

Row 34: P all sts.

Row 35: K all sts.

Using yarn B, bind off purlwise.

Finishing
Weave in the ends and press gently. Backstitch the seam and turn the hat right side out. Thread yarn A through the lace holes at the top of the crown. Draw up tightly and weave in the ends.

The russet tones of this hat will look great in the fall, or you could try shades of yellow and green for a springtime beanie.

Project 13: Warm winter muff

This project involves no shaping at all, so it is a fun and easy alternative to gloves, and can be adapted for a child by simply reducing the number of stitches and length of the knitting. The fur-effect yarn gives the muff a warm, cozy, and wonderfully textured look.

before you start

Measurements

One size to fit average-sized woman's hands

Materials

Yarn A 2 x 2oz (50g) balls (approx. 22yds/20m per ball) super bulky-weight mohair/wool mix fur-effect yarn

Yarn B 1 x 2oz (50g) ball (approx. 93yds/85m per ball) bulky-weight angora/extra fine merino mix yarn

Needles

1 pair size 11 (8mm) needles

Gauge

Yarn A—9 sts x 10 rows to 4in (10cm) measured over reverse stockinette stitch using size 11 (8mm) needles

Yarn B—11 sts x 13 rows to 4in (10cm) measured over stockinette stitch using size 11 (8mm) needles

Abbreviations

k—knit; p—purl; patt—pattern; rs—right side; sl—slip stitch knitwise from left to right needle without working it; st(s)—stitch(es); ws—wrong side

Knitting the muff

Using size 11 (8mm) needles and yarn A, cast on 26 sts.

Fur tube

Row 1 (rs): P all sts.
Row 2: Sl 1, k to last st, sl 1.
Continue patt as established by rows 1 and 2 until work measures 15in (38cm), ending with a ws row. Bind off knitwise and weave in the ends.

Cuffs (make 2)

With rs of muff facing, use size 11 (8mm) needles and yarn B to pick up 30 sts down side edge of the fur tube.
Row 1: P2, (k2, p2) to end.

Row 2: K2, (p2, k2) to end.
Rows 3–24: Repeat rows 1 and 2 eleven times. Bind off ribwise.

Finishing

Weave in the ends on the cuffs. Do not press. Fold the muff in half, right sides together, and make sure that the side seams of the cuffs align. Using yarn B, sew the side seams of both cuffs using backstitch. Using yarn A, backstitch the fur tube's side seam. Turn right side out and gently fluff up the fur of the muff by hand.

You could easily attach a cord to the muff to hang it around your neck when not in use. Buy a readymade cord or use a length of braided yarn like the handles of the patchwork bag (see page 62).

Project 14: Funky fingerless gloves and wrist warmers

This simple glove design has been adapted into four different looks: buttoned, striped, and sequinned fingerless gloves, plus striped wrist warmers. For the gloves, the finger section is worked in one piece and then chain stitched to create a separate opening for each finger.

before you start

Measurements

One size to fit average-sized woman's hands

Materials

Buttoned gloves

2 x 2oz (50g) balls (approx. 131yds/120m per ball) DK merino yarn
Eight ⅜in (1cm) square shell buttons

Striped gloves

2oz (50g) balls (approx. 137yds/125m per ball) DK extra fine merino yarn in 3 colors:

Yarn A   Grizzle x 1 ball
Yarn B   Black x 1 ball
Yarn C   Gray x 1 ball

Sequinned gloves

1 x 2oz (50g) ball (approx. 196yds/180m per ball) DK merino/alpaca mix tweed-effect yarn
50 gold sequins

Wrist warmers

2oz (50g) balls (approx. 123yds/113m per ball) DK merino/cotton mix yarn in 4 colors:

Yarn A   Brown x 1 ball
Yarn B   Maroon x 1 ball
Yarn C   Orange x 1 ball
Yarn D   Crimson x 1 ball

Needles

1 pair size 3 (3.25mm) needles
1 pair size 5 (3.75mm) needles

Gauge

Fingerless gloves—22 sts x 32 rows to 4in (10cm) measured over stockinette stitch using size 5 (3.75mm) needles.
Wrist warmers—24 sts x 30 rows to 4in (10cm) measured over stockinette stitch using size 5 (3.75mm) needles

Abbreviations

k—knit; m1—make 1 stitch by picking up horizontal bar before next stitch, putting it onto left needle, then knitting into back of it; p—purl; rem—remaining; rs—right side; seq 1—place 1 sequin; st(s)—stitch(es); ws—wrong side

These fingerless gloves with button detail are great for outdoor activities when you need to keep warm but want your fingers to stay free.

Buttoned gloves (make 2)

Using size 3 (3.25mm) needles, cast on 42 sts.

Row 1 (rs): P1, (k2, p2) to last st, p1.

Row 2: K1, (k2, p2) to last st, k1.

Rows 3–34: Repeat rows 1 and 2 sixteen times.

Change to size 5 (3.75mm) needles.

Rows 35–46: Beginning with a k row, work 12 rows in stockinette stitch.

Shaping the thumb gusset

Row 47 (rs): K20, m1, k2, m1, k20 (44 sts).

Row 48 and all ws rows: P all sts.

Row 49: K all sts.

Row 51: K20, m1, k4, m1, k20 (46 sts).

Row 53: K all sts.

Row 55: K20, m1, k6, m1, k20 (48 sts).

Row 57: K all sts.

Row 59: K20, m1, k8, m1, k20 (50 sts).

Row 61: K all sts.

Row 63: K20, m1, k10, m1, k20 (52 sts).

Row 65: K32 and turn.

Knitting the thumb

Next row (ws): Cast on 1 st, p this st, p12, turn (13 sts).

Next row: Cast on 3 sts, k these 3 sts, k13 (16 sts).

Beginning with a p row, work another 4 rows in stockinette stitch on these 16 sts only, ending with rs facing. Bind off knitwise and backstitch the thumb seam.

Finger section

**With rs facing, rejoin yarn to rem sts. Pick up and k3 sts previously cast on at base of thumb, then k to end (43 sts).

Row 66 (ws): P all sts.

Rows 67–76: Beginning with a k row, work 10 rows in stockinette stitch.

Row 77: K5, (m1, k4) 4 times, (m1, k1) twice, (m1, k4) 5 times (54 sts).

Row 78: K1, p4, (k1, p6) 3 times, k2, (p6, k1) 3 times, p4, k1.

Row 79: P1, k4, (p1, k6) 3 times, p2, (k6, p1) 3 times, k4, p1.

Rows 80–83: Repeat rows 78 and 79 twice.

Row 84: Repeat row 78. Bind off knitwise.

Striped gloves (make 2)

Using size 3 (3.25mm) needles and yarn A, cast on 42 sts.

Row 1 (rs): P1, (k2, p2) to last 3 sts, k2, p1.

Row 2: K1, (p2, k2) to last 3 sts, p2, k1.

Without breaking off yarn A, join yarn B.

Rows 3–4: Using yarn B, repeat rows 1 and 2.

Without breaking off yarn B, join yarn C.

Rows 5–6: Using yarn C, repeat rows 1 and 2.

Rows 7–34: Continue pattern as established by rows 1–6, maintaining the stripe sequence.

Change to size 5 (3.75mm) needles and remember to keep stripe sequence correct throughout all following rows.

Rows 35–46: Beginning with a k row, work 12 rows in stockinette stitch.

Follow the instructions for the buttoned gloves from row 47 to end.

TIP: WORKING WITH MULTIPLE YARNS

Do not break off yarns when working in stripes but carry the yarns not in use up the side of the glove. This cuts down on the number of ends to be woven in afterward.

Whoever said you shouldn't mix stripes with stripes? These horizontally striped fingerless gloves look great teamed with a vertically striped shirt.

Sequinned gloves

RIGHT GLOVE

Thread 25 sequins onto the yarn. Using size 3 (3.25mm) needles, cast on 42 sts.
Rows 1–20: Follow instructions for rows 1–20 of buttoned gloves.
Change to size 5 (3.75mm) needles.
Rows 21–32: Beginning with a k row, work 12 rows of stockinette stitch +*+.

Thumb gusset and sequins

Row 33 (rs): K6, (seq 1, k1) 5 times, k4, m1, k2, m1, k20 (44 sts).
Row 34 and all ws rows: P all sts.
Row 35: K all sts.
Row 37: K5, (seq 1, k1) 5 times, k5, m1, k4, m1, k20 (46 sts).
Row 39: K all sts.
Row 41: K6, (seq 1, k1) 5 times, k4, m1, k6, m1, k20 (48 sts).
Row 43: K all sts.
Row 45: K5, (seq 1, k1) 5 times, k5, m1, k8, m1, k20 (50 sts).
Row 47: K all sts.
Row 49: K6, (seq 1, k1) 5 times, k4, m1, k10, m1, k20 (52 sts).
Row 51: K32 and turn.

Thumb and finger section

Next row (ws): Cast on 1 st, p this stitch, p12, turn (13 sts).
Next row: Cast on 3 sts, k these 3 sts, k13 (16 sts).
Beginning with a p row, work another 4 rows in stockinette stitch on these 16 sts only, ending with rs facing. Bind off knitwise and backstitch the thumb seam.

To work the finger section, follow the instructions for the buttoned gloves from ** to end.

LEFT GLOVE

Follow the instructions for right glove to +*+.

Thumb gusset and sequins

Row 33 (rs): K20, m1, k2, m1, k5, (seq 1, k1) 5 times, k5 (44 sts).
Row 34 and all ws rows: P all sts.
Row 35: K all sts.
Row 37: K20, m1, k4, m1, k6, (seq 1, k1) 5 times, k4 (46 sts).
Row 39: K all sts.
Row 41: K20, m1, k6, m1, k5, (seq 1, k1) 5 times, k5 (48 sts).
Row 43: K all sts.
Row 45: K20, m1, k8, m1, k6, (seq 1, k1) 5 times, k4 (50 sts).
Row 47: K all sts.
Row 49: K20, m1, k10, m1, k5, (seq 1, k1) 5 times, k5 (52 sts).
Row 51: K32 and turn.
Complete as for the right glove.

FINISHING (ALL GLOVES)

Weave in the ends. Fold each glove right sides facing and sew the side seam using backstitch. Turn right side out and align the ridges made by the purl stitches on the finger section, back and front. Sew together using chain stitch to complete the four "fingers." Sew 3 buttons down the side of each buttoned glove. Press gently, but do not press the ribbing.

TIP: PLACING SEQUINS

Thread sequins onto the yarn and place them in your knitting using the same technique as for adding beads (see page 41).

Add sparkle to your fingerless gloves with sequins in a complementary color.

Wrist warmers (make 2)

Using size 5 (3.75mm) needles and yarn B, cast on 41 sts.

Row 1 (rs): P2, (k1, p2) to end. Break off yarn B.

Row 2: Using yarn C, k2, (p1, k2) to end. Break off yarn C.

Row 3: Using yarn D, p2, (k1, p2) to end. Break off yarn D.

Row 4: Using yarn A, k2, (p1, k2) to end.

Row 5: Still using yarn A, p2, (k1, p2) to end.

Rows 6–11: Repeat rows 4 and 5 three times, then break off yarn A.

Row 12: Using yarn B, k2, (p1, k2) to end. Break off yarn B.

Row 13: Using yarn C, p2, (k1, p2) to end. Break off yarn C.

Row 14: Using yarn D, k2, (p1, k2) to end. Break off yarn D.

Row 15: Using yarn A, p2, (k1, p2) to end.

Row 16: Still using yarn A, k2, (p1, k2) to end.

Rows 17–22: Repeat rows 15 and 16 three times.

Rows 23–36: Repeat rows 1–14 once. Break off yarn A. Using yarn D, bind off ribwise.

Finishing

Weave in the ends and backstitch the side seams. Do not press.

Project 15: Pretty floral bag

The main fabric of this brightly colored bag is knitted with a random-dyed cotton yarn that produces a striped effect, making each bag unique. Personalize your bag with as many or as few beads as you like.

before you start

Measurements

11in (28cm) wide x 1¼in (3cm) deep x 7in (18cm) high

Materials

Yarn A   3 x 2oz (50g) balls (approx. 76yds/70m per ball) DK random-dyed cotton yarn

Yarn B   1 x 2oz (50g) ball (approx. 93yds/85m per ball) DK cream-colored cotton yarn

Approx. 120 small colored beads

Two 27in (69cm) lengths beige eyelet trim

Two 15in (38cm) x 8¾in (22cm) pieces fabric in a complementary color for lining

Needles

1 pair size 5 (3.75mm) needles

1 pair size 5 (3.75mm) double-pointed needles

Gauge

21 sts x 30 rows to 4in (10cm) measured over stockinette stitch using size 5 (3.75mm) needles

Abbreviations

inc 1—increase 1 stitch by knitting into front and back of next stitch on a knit row, or purling into front and back of next stitch on a purl row; k—knit; k2tog—knit 2 stitches together; p—purl; rs—right side; st(s)—stitch(es); tbl—through back of loop; ws—wrong side

Knitting the bag
Panels (make 2)

Using size 5 (3.75mm) needles and yarn A, cast on 62 sts. Work from the chart on page 81, placing flowers as indicated. Use a different bobbin of yarn B for each flower motif, but the same ball of yarn A for the main fabric area. Join each bobbin of yarn B into the knitting using the intarsia technique, but use the fairisle technique to carry the yarns across the backs of the flowers (see pages 32–33). Shape the sides of the panels as indicated on the chart. Increase at the beginning or end of a row using inc 1. Decrease at the beginning of a row by k2tog tbl; decrease at the end of a row by k2tog. When the final row of the chart has been completed, bind off knitwise.

Ties (make 2)

Using size 5 (3.75mm) double-pointed needles and yarn A, cast on 4 sts and knit the i-cord until it measures 11in (28cm) long. Finish the cord, leaving a long end of yarn for sewing it to the bag.

Handles (make 2)

Cut two 47in (120cm) lengths of yarn A and knot together at one end. Tape the knotted end to a stable surface such as a table and, holding the other end between your finger and thumb, twist the two ends as tightly as possible, then fold in half. Tie all four ends together and then smooth out the cord so that the twist is evenly distributed.

Use a sewing machine to stitch ¼in (5mm) in from the raw edge of the eyelet trim to neaten. Thread the twisted cord through the eyelets and knot at each end on the wrong side to secure.

New skills:
knitting i-cord

I-cord is very easy to knit using double-pointed needles. If you find that you work a lot with i-cords, invest in a knitting mill—it saves time.

1 Cast on the required number of stitches and knit 1 row. Slide the stitches along the right needle from the left to the right tip. Transfer this needle to your left hand, so that the working end of the yarn is coming from the bottom stitch on the needle.

2 Knit the next row, pulling the yarn tightly across the back of the stitches as you do so. Repeat this process until the cord is the required length. Cut the yarn, thread it through all the stitches, and fasten securely.

1

2

Knitted accessories aren't just for winter. This floral bag is perfect for a summer picnic, garden party, or an informal outdoor wedding.

TIP: ALTERNATIVE MATERIALS

If you cannot find any random-dyed yarn, buy several balls of different colored yarn and knit the stripes with these. You can knit stripes of equal size or vary them if you prefer. If you cannot find any readymade eyelet trim, buy some fabric and an eyelet punch to make your own.

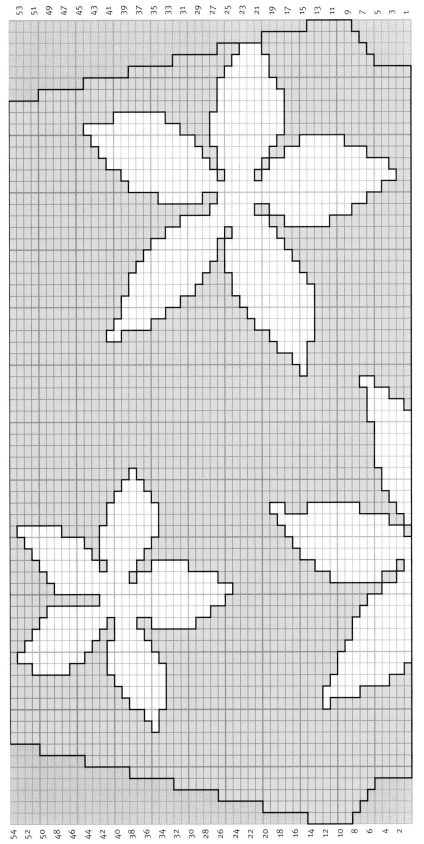

Column numbers (top): 53 51 49 47 45 43 41 39 37 35 33 31 29 27 25 23 21 19 17 15 13 11 9 7 5 3 1

Column numbers (bottom): 54 52 50 48 46 44 42 40 38 36 34 32 30 28 26 24 22 20 18 16 14 12 10 8 6 4 2

FINISHING
Bag
Weave in the ends, press the pieces carefully on the wrong side, and allow to cool. With right sides facing, backstitch the bottom seam of the bag. Using a sewing needle and thread, bead the centers of each flower. With right sides facing, match up the top edges and bottom corners and backstitch the side seams (rows 9–54). Flatten the bag from the side seams toward the base seam, then backstitch the remaining seams at the bottom corners.

Handles
Positioning the handles 2in (5cm) in from each side seam and 1in (2.5cm) below the top edge, sew securely in place.

Lining
Cut the two fabric pieces of the lining to the same size and shape as the knitted panels, adding a 1in (2.5cm) seam allowance all around. With right sides together, sew the base seam using a sewing machine or needle and thread. Match up the top edges and sew the side seams from top edge to bottom corners (rows 9–54). Flatten the lining from the side seams toward the base seam and sew the remaining seams at the bottom corners. Fold down the top edges and press the hem to the wrong side. Trim the seam allowances for a less bulky finish, then place the lining inside the bag, with the wrong sides of the lining and bag facing. Overcast the pressed hem of the lining to the top edge of the bag.

TIP: CARRYING THE YARNS
Although you could make this bag entirely by intarsia, using the fairisle technique to carry the yarns across the back of the flowers will reduce the number of ends to be woven in when you have finished.

KEY ▨ Yarn A—k on rs, p on ws   ▢ Yarn B—k on rs, p on ws   ▨ Stitch not in work due to shaping

Project 16: Ribbed earflap hat

This snug hat is worked in an irregular brioche ribbing pattern on a background of reverse stockinette stitch, which makes the ribbing more pronounced. The edging of contrasting colored yarn is an attractive finishing touch.

before you start

Measurements One size to fit average-sized woman's head

Materials 2 x 2oz (50g) balls (approx. 95yds/87m per ball) Aran-weight extra fine merino yarn
Scrap of same yarn in a contrasting color

Needles 1 pair size 7 (4.5mm) needles

Gauge 21 sts x 27 rows to 4in (10cm) measured over reverse stockinette stitch using size 7 (4.5mm) needles

Abbreviations k—knit; k1b—work next stitch by inserting needle into stitch on row below and knit it together with stitch above; k2tog—knit 2 stitches together; m1—make 1 stitch by picking up horizontal bar before next stitch, putting it onto left needle, then purling into back of it; m2—make 2 stitches by picking up horizontal bar before next stitch, putting it onto left needle, then purling into back and front of it; p—purl; p2tog—purl 2 stitches together; rem—remaining; rs—right side; st(s)—stitch(es); tbl—through back of loop; ws—wrong side

Knitting the hat

Using size 7 (4.5mm) needles and the main yarn, cast on 18 sts.
Row 1 (rs): P all sts.
Row 2 and all ws rows: K all sts.
Row 3: (P3, m1) twice, p3, m2, (p3, m1) twice, p3 (24 sts).
Row 5: (P4, m1) twice, p4, m2, (p4, m1) twice, p4 (30 sts).
Row 7: (P5, m1) twice, p5, m2, (p5, m1) twice, p5 (36 sts).
Row 9: (P6, m1) twice, p6, m2, (p6, m1) twice, p6 (42 sts).
Row 11: (P7, m1) twice, p7, m2, (p7, m1)

wice, p7 (48 sts).
Row 13: (P8, m1) twice, p8, m2, (p8, m1) twice, p8 (54 sts).
Row 15: (P9, m1) twice, p9, m2, (p9, m1) twice, p9 (60 sts).
Row 17: (P10, m1) twice, p10, m2, (p10, m1) twice, p10 (66 sts).
Row 19: (P11, m1) twice, p11, m2, (p11, m1) twice, p11 (72 sts).
Row 21: (P12, m1) twice, p12, m2, (p12, m1) twice, p12 (78 sts).
Row 23: (P13, m1) twice, p13, m2, (p13, m1) twice, p13 (84 sts).
Row 25: (P14, m1) twice, p14, m2, (p14,

m1) twice, p14 (90 sts).
Row 27: (P15, m1) twice, p15, m2, (p15, m1) twice, p15 (96 sts).
Row 29: (P16, m1) 5 times, p to end (101 sts).
Row 31: P all sts.
Row 33: P all sts.
Row 35: P10, k1, p7, k1, p15, k1, (p7, k1) 4 times, p15, k1, p7, k1, p to end.
Row 36: K10, p1, k7, p1, k15, p1, (k7, p1) 4 times, k15, p1, k7, p1, k to end.
Row 37: P10, k1b, p7, k1b, p15, k1b, (p7, k1b) 4 times, p15, k1b, p7, k1b, p to end.
Rows 38–39: Repeat rows 36 and 37.
Row 40: Repeat row 36.
Row 41: P2tog, p8, k1b, p7, k1b, p15, k1b, (p7, k1b) 4 times, p15, k1b, p7, k1b, p to last 2 sts, p2tog (99 sts).
Row 42: K9, p1, k7, p1, k15, p1, (k7, p1) 4 times, k15, p1, k7, p1, k to end.
Row 43: P9, k1b, p7, k1b, p15, k1b, (p7, k1b) 4 times, p15, k1b, p7, k1b, p to end.
Row 44: Repeat row 42.
Row 45: P5, (k1, p3, k1b, p3) twice, k1, p7, (k1, p3, k1b, p3) 5 times, k1, p7, (k1, p3, k1b, p3) twice, k1, p to end.
Row 46: K5, p1, (k3, p1) 4 times, k7, p1, (k3, p1) 10 times, k7, p1, (k3, p1) 4 times, k to end.
Rows 47–48: Repeat rows 45 and 46.
Row 49: P2tog, (p3, k1b) 5 times, p7, k1b, (p3, k1b) 10 times, p7, k1b, (p3, k1b) 4 times, p to last 2 sts, p2tog (97 sts).
Row 50: K4, p1, (k3, p1) 4 times, k7, (p1, k3) 10 times, p1, k7, (p1, k3) 4 times, p1, k to end.
Row 51: P4, (k1b, p3) 4 times, k1b, p7, (k1b, p3) 10 times, k1b, p7, (k1b, p3) 4 times, k1b, p to end.
Rows 52–53: Repeat rows 50 and 51.

With its pointed tip and earflap ties, this hat is perfect for the pixie look. The contrast edging frames the face beautifully.

Row 54: Repeat row 50.

Row 55: P4, (k1b, p3) 5 times, k1, (p3, k1b) 11 times, p3, k1, (p3, k1b) 5 times, p to end.

Row 56: K4, p1, (k3, p1) to last 4 sts, k4.

Dividing for earflaps

Next row (rs): Break off yarn. Slip first 34 sts onto a stitch holder. Bind off the center 29 sts knitwise using contrast yarn, then break off yarn. Rejoin main yarn to rem sts, p1, k1b, (p3, k1b) 7 times, p2, p2tog (33 sts).

Next row: (K3, p1) to last st, k1.

Left earflap

Row 1: P1, (k1b, p3) to end.

Row 2: (K3, p1) to last st, k1.

Row 3: Repeat row 1, then break off yarn.

Row 4: Using contrast yarn, bind off first 14 sts purlwise. Rejoin main yarn to rem 19 sts, k1, p1, (k3, p1) to last st, k1.

**Row 5: P1, (k1b, p3) to last 2 sts, k1b, p1.

Row 6: K1, p1, (k3, p1) to last st, k1.

Rows 7–10: Repeat rows 5 and 6 twice.

Row 11: K2tog tbl, p3, (k1b, p3) to last 2 sts, k2tog (17 sts).

Row 12: (P1, k3) to last st, p1.

Row 13: (K1, p3) to last st, k1.

Rows 14–15: Repeat rows 12 and 13.

Row 16: Repeat row 12.

Row 17: K2tog tbl, p2, (k1b, p3) twice, k1b, p2, k2tog (15 sts).

Row 18: P1, k2, (p1, k3) twice, p1, k2, p1.

Row 19: K1, p2, (k1b, p3) twice, k1b, p2, k1.

Row 20: Repeat row 18.

Row 21: K2tog tbl, p1, (k1b, p3) twice, k1b, p1, k2tog (13 sts).

Row 22: P1, k1, (p1, k3) twice, p1, k1, p1.

Row 23: K2tog tbl, (k1b, p3) twice, k1b, k2tog (11 sts).

Row 24: P2, k3, p1, k3, p2.

Row 25: K2tog tbl, p3, k1b, p3, k2tog (9 sts).

Row 26: P2tog, k2, p1, k2, p2tog tbl (7 sts).

Row 27: K2tog tbl, p1, k1b, p1, k2tog (5 sts). Bind off purlwise.

Right earflap

With rs facing, pick up sts from holder and rejoin main yarn.

Row 1 (rs): P2tog, p2, (k1b, p3) to last 2 sts, k1b, p1 (33 sts).

Row 2: K1, (p1, k3) to end.

Row 3: (P3, k1b) to last st, p1.

Rows 4–5: Repeat rows 2 and 3.

Row 6: Repeat row 2, then break off yarn.

Row 7: Using contrast yarn, bind off first 14 sts, then break off yarn. Rejoin main yarn to rem sts and work as for left earflap from ** to end.

Finishing

Weave in the ends and backstitch the back seam very neatly. Steam gently, taking care not to flatten the texture of the knitting. Using contrast yarn, chain stitch along the edge of the earflaps to join up with the contrast stitches around the edge of the hat. For each tie, cut six 49in (124cm) lengths of main yarn. Fold each piece in half and use a crochet hook to thread three of them through the tip of each earflap on the wrong side. Braid the three doubled ends together loosely and secure with a knot 3¼in (8cm) from the end.

Project 17: Slouching socks

These socks are ideal for relaxing in. Unlike most socks, which are knitted on sets of double-pointed needles, these are worked on just two single-pointed needles, making them easier to knit. The ribbing that slants from the side edges toward the center stops at the heel to make shaping simple to follow.

before you start

Measurements
One size to fit average-sized woman's feet

Materials
2 x 2oz (50g) balls (approx. 175yds/160m per ball) Aran-weight cotton/acrylic mix yarn

Needles
1 pair size 5 (3.75mm) needles
1 pair size 6 (4mm) needles

Gauge
26 sts x 33 rows to 4in (10cm) measured over stockinette stitch using size 6 (4mm) needles

Abbreviations
inc 1—increase/increasing 1 stitch by purling into front and back of next stitch; k—knit; k2tog—knit 2 stitches together; p—purl; p2tog—purl 2 stitiches together; rs—right side; st(s)—stitch(es); tbl—through back of loop; ws—wrong side

Knitting the socks (make 2)
Using size 5 (3.75mm) needles, cast on 64 sts.
Row 1 (rs): P1, (k2, p2) to last 3 sts, k2, p1.
Row 2: K1, (p2, k2) to last 3 sts, p2, k1.
Rows 3–5: Repeat rows 1 and 2, then repeat row 1.
Row 6: Inc 1, (k2, p2) to last st, inc 1 (66 sts).
Change to size 6 (4mm) needles.
Row 7: P2, (k2, p2) to end.
Row 8: K2, (p2, k2) to end.
Rows 9–16: Repeat rows 7 and 8 four times.
Row 17: P2tog, p1, (k2, p2) 7 times, k4, (p2, k2) 7 times, p1, p2tog (64 sts).
Row 18: (K2, p2) 7 times, k2, p4, k2, (p2, k2) 7 times.
Row 19: (P2, k2) 7 times, p2, k4, p2, (k2, p2) 7 times.
Row 20: (K2, p2) 7 times, k2, p4, k2, (p2, k2) 7 times.
Rows 21–26: Repeat rows 19 and 20 three times.
Row 27: P2tog, p1, (k2, p2) to last 5 sts, k2, p1, p2tog (62 sts).
Row 28: K2, (p2, k2) to end.
Row 29: P2, (k2, p2) to end.
Row 30: K2, (p2, k2) to end.

Rows 31–36: Repeat rows 29 and 30 three times.
Row 37: P2tog, p1, (k2, p2) 6 times, k2, p4, k2, (p2, k2) 6 times, p1, p2tog (60 sts).
Row 38: (K2, p2) 7 times, k4, (p2, k2) 7 times.
Row 39: (P2, k2) 7 times, p4, (k2, p2) 7 times.
Row 40: (K2, p2) 7 times, k4, (p2, k2) 7 times.
Rows 41–46: Repeat rows 39 and 40 three times.
Row 47: P2tog, p1, (k2, p2) to last 5 sts, k2, p1, p2tog (58 sts).
Row 48: K2, (p2, k2) to end.
Row 49: P2, (k2, p2) to end.
Row 50: K2, (p2, k2) to end.
Rows 51–56: Repeat rows 49 and 50 three times.
Row 57: P2tog, p1, (k2, p2) 6 times, k4, (p2, k2) 6 times, p1, p2tog (56 sts).
Row 58: (K2, p2) 6 times, k2, p4, k2, (p2, k2) 6 times.
Row 59: (P2, k2) 6 times, p2, k4, p2, (k2, p2) 6 times.
Row 60: (K2, p2) 6 times, k2, p4, k2, (p2, k2) 6 times.
Rows 61–66: Repeat rows 59 and 60 three times.

Row 67: P2tog, p1, (k2, p2) to last 5 sts, k2, p1, p2tog (54 sts).

Row 68: K2, (p2, k2) to end.

Row 69: P2, (k2, p2) to end.

Row 70: K2, (p2, k2) to end.

Rows 71–76: Repeat rows 69 and 70 three times.

Row 77: P2tog, p1, (k2, p2) 5 times, k2, p4, k2, (p2, k2) 5 times, p1, p2tog (52 sts).

Row 78: (K2, p2) 6 times, k4, (p2, k2) 6 times.

Row 79: (P2, k2) 6 times, p4, (k2, p2) 6 times.

Row 80: (K2, p2) 6 times, k4, (p2, k2) 6 times.

Rows 81–86: Repeat rows 79 and 80 three times.

Shaping the heel

Row 87 (rs): K13 and turn.

Row 88 and all ws rows: P all sts.

Row 89: K12 and turn.

Row 91: K11 and turn.

Row 93: K10 and turn.

Row 95: K9 and turn.

Row 97: K8 and turn.

Row 99: K7 and turn.

Row 101: K6 and turn.

Row 103: K5 and turn.

Row 105: K6 and turn.

Row 107: K7 and turn.

Row 109: K8 and turn.

Row 111: K9 and turn.

Row 113: K10 and turn.

Row 115: K11 and turn.

Row 117: K12 and turn.

Row 119: K13 and turn.

Row 121: K13, p2, (k2, p2) to last st, k1.

Row 122: P13 and turn.

Row 123 and all rs rows: K all sts.

Row 124: P12 and turn.

Row 126: P11 and turn.

Row 128: P10 and turn.

Row 130: P9 and turn.

Row 132: P8 and turn.

Row 134: P7 and turn.

Row 136: P6 and turn.

Row 138: P5 and turn.

Row 140: P6 and turn.

Row 142: P7 and turn.

Row 144: P8 and turn.

Row 146: P9 and turn.

Row 148: P10 and turn.

Row 150: P11 and turn.

Row 152: P12 and turn.

Row 154: P13 and turn.

Row 156: P13, (k2, p2) 6 times, k2, p13.

Knitting the foot

Row 157: K13, (p2, k2) 6 times, p2, k13.

Row 158: P13, (k2, p2) 6 times, k2, p13.

Repeat rows 157 and 158 until foot measures 6in (15cm) from end of heel shaping, ending with rs facing for next row.

Shaping the toe

Row 1 (rs): K10, k2tog, k2, k2tog tbl, k1, (p2, k2) 4 times, p2, k1, k2tog, k2, k2tog tbl, k10 (48 sts).

Row 2: P15, (k2, p2) 4 times, k2, p15.

Row 3: K9, k2tog, k2, k2tog tbl, (p2, k2) 4 times, p2, k2tog, k2, k2tog tbl, k9 (44 sts).

Row 4: P13, (k2, p2) 4 times, k2, p13.

Row 5: K8, k2tog, k2, k2tog tbl, p1, (k2, p2) 3 times, k2, p1, k2tog, k2, k2tog tbl, k8 (40 sts).

Row 6: P12, k1, (p2, k2) 3 times, p2, k1, p12.

Row 7: K7, k2tog, k2, k2tog tbl, (k2, p2) 3 times, k2, k2tog, k2, k2tog tbl, k7 (36 sts).

Row 8: P13, (k2, p2) twice, k2, p13.

Row 9: K6, k2tog, k2, k2tog tbl, k1, (p2, k2) twice, p2, k1, k2tog, k2, k2tog tbl, k6 (32 sts).

Row 10: P11, (k2, p2) twice, k2, p11.

Row 11: K5, k2tog, k2, k2tog tbl, (p2, k2) twice, p2, k2tog, k2, k2tog tbl, k5 (28 sts).

Row 12: P9, (k2, p2) twice, k2, p9.

Row 13: K4, k2tog, k2, k2tog tbl, p1, k2, p2, k2, p1, k2tog, k2, k2tog tbl, k4 (24 sts).

Row 14: P8, k1, p2, k2, p2, k1, p8. Bind off knitwise.

Finishing

Weave in the ends. Fold each sock so that right sides are facing and sew the long seam using backstitch. Turn each sock right side out and fold so that the seam is at the center back. Overcast the toe seam on the right side. Do not press.

These thick calf-length socks will keep your feet warm and cozy, and are perfect for wearing around the house on a lazy Sunday morning.

Project 18: Cabled mittens

These mittens are worked in reverse stockinette stitch with a traveling cable on the back. They are knitted in a luxurious angora/extra fine merino mix yarn, making them really comfy to wear.

before you start

Measurements One size to fit average-sized woman's hands

Materials 2 x 2oz (50g) balls (approx. 120yds/110m per ball) bulky-weight anglora/extra fine merino mix yarn

Needles 1 pair size 7 (4.5mm) needles
1 pair size 8 (5mm) needles
1 cable needle

Gauge 18 sts x 25 rows to 4in (10cm) measured over stockinette stitch using size 8 (5mm) needles

Abbreviations c6b—cable 6 back; c6f—cable 6 front; k—knit; k2tog—knit 2 stitches together; m1—make 1 stitch by picking up horizontal bar before next stitch, putting it onto left needle, then purling into back of it; p—purl; p2tog—purl 2 stitches together; rem—remaining; rs—right side; st(s)—stitch(es); tbl—through back of loop; ws—wrong side

Knitting the mittens
RIGHT MITTEN
Using size 7 (4.5mm) needles, cast on 37 sts.
Row 1 (rs): P1, (k1, p1) to end.
Row 2: K1, (p1, k1) to end.
Rows 3–14: Repeat rows 1 and 2 six times. Change to size 8 (5mm) needles.
Row 15: (P1, k1) 3 times, p11, k1, p1, k1, p to end.
Row 16: K17, p1, k1, p1, k11, (p1, k1) 3 times.
Rows 17–18: Repeat rows 15 and 16.

Shaping the thumb gusset
Row 19: (P1, k1) 3 times, p11, k1, m1, p1, m1, k1, p to end (39 sts).
Row 20: K17, p2, k1, p2, k11, (p1, k1) 3 times.
Row 21: (P1, k1) 3 times, p11, k1, m1, k1, p1, k1, m1, k1, p to end (41 sts).
Row 22: K17, (p1, k1) 3 times, p1, k11, (p1, k1) 3 times.
Row 23: (P1, k1) 3 times, p11, k1, m1, (p1, k1) twice, p1, m1, k1, p to end (43 sts).
Row 24: K17, p1, k2, p1, k1, p1, k2, p1, k11, (p1, k1) 3 times.
Row 25: (P1, k1) 3 times, p11, k1, m1, p2, k1, p1, k1, p2, m1, k1, p to end (45 sts).
Row 26: K17, p1, k3, p1, k1, p1, k3, p1, p11, (p1, k1) 3 times.
Row 27: (P1, k1) 3 times, p11, k1, m1, p3, k1, p1, k1, p3, m1, k1, p to end (47 sts).
Row 28: K17, p1, k4, p1, k1, p1, k4, p1, k11, (p1, k1) 3 times.
Row 29: P1, c6b, p1, k1, p8, k1, m1, p4, k1, p1, k1, p4, m1, k1, p to end (49 sts).
Row 30: K17, p1, k5, p1, k1, p1, k5, p1, k8, (p1, k1) twice, p1, k to end.
Row 31: P3, (p1, k1) 3 times, p8, k1, p5, k1, p1, k1, p5, turn.

Knitting the thumb
Next row (ws): K5, p1, k1, p1, k5, turn (13 sts).
Next row (rs): P5, k1, p1, k1, p5, turn. Continuing on these 13 sts only, repeat the previous two rows seven times.
Break off yarn, leaving enough to sew the thumb seam, and thread the yarn through the sts. Pull up tight and fasten securely. Backstitch the thumb seam.

Finger section

With rs facing, rejoin yarn to rem sts, pick up and p2 sts at base of thumb, k1, p to end (38 sts).

Row 32 (ws): K17, p1, k2, p1, k8, (p1, k1) 3 times, k to end.

Row 33: P3, (p1, k1) 3 times, p8, k1, p2, k1, p to end.

Row 34: K17, p1, k2, p1, k8, (p1, k1) 3 times, k to end.

Rows 35–38: Repeat rows 33 and 34 twice.

Row 39: P4, c6b, p1, k1, p5, k1, p2, k1, p to end.

Row 40: K17, p1, k2, p1, k5, (p1, k1) 3 times, k to end.

Row 41: P6, (p1, k1) 3 times, p5, k1, p2, k1, p to end.

Row 42: K17, p1, k2, p1, k5, (p1, k1) 3 times, k to end.

Rows 43–48: Repeat rows 41 and 42 three times.

Row 49: P7, c6b, p1, k1, (p2, k1) twice, p to end.

Row 50: K17, (p1, k2) twice, (p1, k1) 3 times, k to end.

Row 51: P10, (k1, p1) 3 times, p1, k1, p2, k1, p to end.

Row 52: K17, (p1, k2) twice, (p1, k1) 3 times, k to end.

Shaping top of mitten

Row 53 (rs): P2tog, p8, (k1, p1) 3 times, k2tog, p2, k2tog tbl, p to last 2 sts, p2tog (34 sts).

Row 54: K15, p1, k2, p1, (k1, p1) 3 times, k to end.

Row 55: P2tog, p7, (k1, p1) twice, k1, k2tog, p2, k2tog tbl, p to last 2 sts, p2tog (30 sts).

Row 56: K13, p1, k2, p1, (p1, k1) 3 times, k to end.

New skills: cabling

A cable is made by crossing one set of stitches over another. In this project, the cables on each mitten are worked so that they move toward each other across the fabric. In order to work the cable, a third (cable) needle is used to hold the stitches to be moved, either at the back or front of the work, depending on the direction in which the cable is moving.

Cable 6 back (c6b)

1 This cable moves to the right. Slip the next 3 sts purlwise off the left needle onto the cable needle and hold the cable needle at the back of the work. Purl the next 3 sts from the left needle as normal.

2 Bring the cable needle into knitting position and k1, p1, k1 from the cable needle. You have now finished with the cable needle. Continue the row working from the left needle as instructed in the pattern.

Cable 6 front (c6f)

3 This cable moves to the left. Slip the next 3 sts purlwise off the left needle onto the cable needle and hold the cable needle at the front of the work. K1, p1, k1 from the left needle. Bring the cable needle into knitting position and purl 3 sts from the cable needle. You have now finished with the cable needle. Continue the row working from the left needle as instructed in the pattern.

Cabling may look complicated but is actually very easy to learn. Once you've got the hang of it, you could try out different cable effects to add your textural interest to your accessories.

Row 57: P2tog, p6, (k1, p1) twice, k2tog, p2, k2tog tbl, p to last 2 sts, p2tog (26 sts).

Row 58: K11, p1, k2, p1, (k1, p1) twice, k to end.

Row 59: P2tog, p5, k1, p1, k1, k2tog, p2, k2tog tbl, p to last 2 sts, p2tog (22 sts).

Row 60: K2tog, k6, p2tog tbl, k2, p2tog, k1, p1, k to last 2 sts, k2tog (18 sts). Bind off rem 18 sts purlwise.

LEFT MITTEN

Work the first 14 rows as for the right mitten.

Row 15: P17, k1, p1, k1, p11, (k1, p1) 3 times.

Row 16: (K1, p1) 3 times, k11, p1, k1, p1, k to end.

Rows 17–18: Repeat rows 15 and 16.

Shaping the thumb gusset

Row 19: P17, k1, m1, p1, m1, k1, p11, (k1, p1) 3 times (39 sts).

Row 20: (K1, p1) 3 times, k11, p2, k1, p2, k to end.

Row 21: P17, k1, m1, k1, p1, k1, m1, k1, p11, (k1, p1) 3 times (41 sts).

Row 22: (K1, p1) 3 times, k11, p1, (k1, p1) 3 times, k to end.

Row 23: P17, k1, m1, p1, (k1, p1) twice, m1, k1, p11, (k1, p1) 3 times (43 sts).

Row 24: (K1, p1) 3 times, k11, p1, k2, p1, k1, p1, k2, p1, k to end.

Row 25: P17, k1, m1, p2, k1, p1, k1, p2, m1, k1, p11, (k1, p1) 3 times (45 sts).

Row 26: (K1, p1) 3 times, k11, p1, k3, p1, k1, p1, k3, p1, k to end.

Row 27: P17, k1, m1, p3, k1, p1, k1, p3, m1, k1, p11, (k1, p1) 3 times (47 sts).

Row 28: (K1, p1) 3 times, k11, p1, k4, p1, k1, p1, k4, p1, k to end.

Row 29: P17, k1, m1, p4, k1, p1, k1, p4, m1, k1, p8, k1, p1, c6f, p1 (49 sts).

Row 30: K4, (p1, k1) 3 times, k7, p1, k5, p1, k1, p1, k5, p1, k to end.

Row 31: P17, k1, p5, k1, p1, k1, p5, turn.

Knitting the thumb

Next row (ws): K5, p1, k1, p1, k5, turn (13 sts).

Next row (rs): P5, k1, p1, k1, p5, turn. Continuing on these 13 sts only, repeat the previous two rows seven times. Break off yarn, leaving enough to sew the thumb seam, and thread the yarn through the stitches. Pull up tight and fasten securely. Backstitch the thumb seam.

Finger section

With rs facing, rejoin yarn to rem sts, pick up and p2 sts at base of thumb, k1, p8, (k1, p1) 3 times, p to end (38 sts).

Row 32 (ws): K4, (p1, k1) 3 times, k7, p1, k2, p1, k to end.

Row 33: P17, k1, p2, k1, p8, (k1, p1) 3 times, p to end.

Row 34: K4, (p1, k1) 3 times, k7, p1, k2, p1, k to end.

Rows 35–38: Repeat rows 33 and 34 twice.

Row 39: P17, k1, p2, k1, p5, k1, p1, c6f, p to end.

Row 40: K7, (p1, k1) 3 times, k4, p1, k2, p1, k to end.

Row 41: P17, k1, p2, k1, p5, (k1, p1) 3 times, p to end.

Row 42: K7, (p1, k1) 3 times, k4, p1, k2, p1, k to end.

Rows 43–48: Repeat rows 41 and 42 three times.

Row 49: P17, (k1, p2) twice, k1, p1, c6f, p to end.

Row 50: K10, (p1, k1) 3 times, k1, p1, k2, p1, k to end.

Row 51: P17, k1, p2, k1, p1, (k1, p1) 3 times, p to end.

Row 52: K10, (p1, k1) 3 times, k1, p1, k2, p1, k to end.

Shaping top of mitten

Row 53 (rs): P2tog, p14, k2tog, p2, k2tog tbl, (p1, k1) 3 times, p to last 2 sts, p2tog.

Row 54: K9, (p1, k1) 3 times, p1, k2, p1, k to end.

Row 55: P2tog, p12, k2tog, p2, k2tog tbl, (k1, p1) twice, k1, p to last 2 sts (30 sts).

Row 56: K8, (p1, k1) twice, p2, k2, p1, k to end.

Row 57: P2tog, p10, k2tog, p2, k2tog tbl, (p1, k1) twice, p to last 2 sts, p2tog (26 sts).

Row 58: K7, (p1, k1) twice, p1, k2, p1, k to end.

Row 59: P2tog, p8, k2tog, p2, k2tog tbl, k1, p1, k1, p to last 2 sts, p2tog (22 sts).

Row 60: K2tog, k4, p1, k1, p2tog tbl, k2, p2tog, k to last 2 sts, k2tog. Bind off rem 18 sts purlwise.

Finishing

Weave in the ends and backstitch the side seams. Press carefully.

Project 19:Rainbow scarf

This colorful scarf has a knitted vent, allowing the other end to pass through in order to fasten snugly around the neck. Achieve the interesting blurred effect by knitting together colored blocks and gently brushing them when finished to blend the different colored fibers.

before you start

Measurements

7in (18cm) wide x 37in (94cm) long

Materials

2oz (50g) balls (approx. 151yds/ 140m per ball) Aran-weight mohair yarn in 3 colors:

Yarn A Purple x 1 ball

Yarn B Pink x 1 ball

Yarn C Orange x 1 ball

1oz (25g) balls (approx. 229yds/ 210m per ball) fingering-weight mohair/silk mix yarn in 2 colors:

Yarn D Blue x 1 ball

Yarn E Green x 1 ball

Yarns D and E are used 4 ends together throughout

Needles

1 pair size 7 (4.5mm) needles

Gauge

20 sts x 25 rows to 4in (10cm) measured over stockinette stitch using size 7 (4.5mm) needles.

Abbreviations

k—knit; p—purl; patt—pattern; rem—remaining; rs—right side; st(s)—stitch(es)

Knitting the scarf

Using yarn C, cast on 40 sts.
Break off yarn C and join yarn A.

Rows 1–6: Using yarn A, k all sts.

Row 7 (rs): K all sts.

Row 8: K5, p30, k5.

Work in patt as established by rows 7 and 8, using yarns indicated.

Rows 9–32: Yarn A.

Rows 33–35: Yarn E.

Rows 36–67: Yarn B.

Rows 68–70: Yarn D.

Rows 71–102: Yarn C.

Rows 103–105: Yarn E.

Rows 106–155: Yarn A.

Rows 156–158: Yarn D.

Rows 159–190: Yarn C.

Rows 191–193: Yarn E.

Row 194: Using yarn B, k5, p12, k6, p12, k5.

Row 195: K all sts.

Row 196: K5, p12, k6, p12, k5.

Making the vent

Row 197: K20 and turn, placing rem sts from left needle onto a stitch holder.

Row 198: K3, p12, k5.

Row 199: K all sts.

Rows 200–214: Repeat rows 198 and 199 seven times, then row 198 once more. Break off yarn.

With rs facing, rejoin yarn B to sts on holder and k all sts. Repeat rows 198–214 to match first side.

Row 215 (rs): K all sts.

Row 216: K5, p12, k6, p12, k5.

Row 217: K all sts.

Row 218: K5, p30, k5.

Row 219: K all sts.

Work in patt as established by rows 218 and 219, using yarns indicated.

Rows 220–229: Yarn B.

Rows 230–232: Yarn D.

Rows 233–258: Yarn A.

Rows 259–264: Using yarn A, k all sts. Using yarn C, bind off knitwise.

Finishing

Weave in the ends and press gently. Fold the scarf in half widthwise and, using a mohair brush or teasel, gently brush away from the fold toward the ends of the scarf so that the colors blend together. Press again using a lot of steam and allow to cool.

This cuddly rainbow scarf will brighten any outfit, is guaranteed to banish the chills, and couldn't be simpler to knit.

Project 20: Driving gloves

The shape of these gloves was inspired by that of leather driving gloves. This pair has been knitted in soft tweed-effect wool. The Swiss-darned embroidery in shimmering gold lurex and the mother-of-pearl buttons give the gloves a feminine touch.

before you start

Measurements

One size to fit average-sized woman's hands

Materials

2oz (50g) balls (approx. 123yds/113m per ball) DK tweed-effect wool yarn in 2 colors:

Yarn A   Dark green x 2 balls

Yarn B   Light green x 1 ball

Yarn C   1 x 1oz (25g) ball (approx. 103yds/95m per ball) fingering-weight gold lurex yarn

2 mother-of-pearl buttons

Needles

1 pair size 5 (3.75mm) needles

Gauge

19 sts x 27 rows to 4in (10cm) measured over stockinette stitch using size 5 (3.75mm) needles

Abbreviations

beg—beginning; k—knit; k2tog—knit 2 stitches together; m1—make 1 stitch by picking up horizontal bar before next stitch, putting it onto left needle, then knitting into back of it; p—purl; rem—remaining; rs—right side; st(s)—stitch(es); ws—wrong side

Knitting the gloves (make 2)

Using size 5 (3.75mm) needles and yarn B, cast on 52 sts.

Rows 1–6: Beginning with a k row, work 6 rows in stockinette stitch. Break off yarn.

Row 7 (rs): Using yarn C, k all sts. Break off yarn.

Row 8: Using yarn A, p all sts. Work all remaining rows in yarn A only.

Row 9: K2tog, k to last 2 sts, k2tog (50 sts).

Row 10: P all sts.

Rows 11–16: Beginning with a k row, work 6 rows in stockinette stitch.

Row 17: K2tog, k to last 2 sts, k2tog (48 sts).

Rows 18–24: Starting with a p row, work 7 rows in stockinette stitch.

Row 25: K2tog, k to last 2 sts, k2tog (46 sts).

Row 26: P all sts.

Shaping the thumb gusset

Row 27 (rs): K22, m1, k2, m1, k22 (48 sts).

Row 28 and all ws rows: P all sts.

Row 29: K22, m1, k4, m1, k22 (50 sts).

Row 31: K22, m1, k6, m1, k22 (52 sts).

Row 33: K22, m1, k8, m1, k22 (54 sts).

Row 35: K32 and turn.

Knitting the thumb

Next row (ws): Cast on 1 st, p this st, p10, turn (11 sts).

Next row: Cast on 3 sts, k these 3 sts, k11, turn (14 sts).

Beginning with a p row, work another 17 rows in stockinette stitch on these 14 sts only, ending with rs facing.

Break off yarn, making sure you leave enough to sew the seam, and thread the yarn through the sts. Pull up tight and fasten securely. Sew the thumb seam using backstitch.

Finger section

With rs facing, rejoin yarn to rem sts. Pick up and k3 sts previously cast on at base of thumb, then k to end (47 sts).

Row 36: P all sts.

Row 37: K2tog, k to last 2 sts, k2tog (45 sts).

Rows 38–44: Beginning with a p row, work another 7 rows in stockinette stitch, ending with rs facing.

Row 45 (rs): K29 and turn.

There are many beautiful metallic yarns available. You could use silver yarn to complement blue gloves, or copper yarn for red ones.

Shaping first finger

Next row (ws): Cast on 1 st, p this st, p13, turn (14 sts).

Next row: Cast on 1 st, k this st, k14 (15 sts).

Beginning with a p row, work another 21 rows in stockinette stitch on these 15 sts only, ending with rs facing.

Break off yarn, making sure you leave enough to sew the seam, and thread the yarn through the sts. Pull up tight and fasten securely. Backstitch the finger seam.

Shaping second finger

With rs facing, rejoin yarn to rem sts.

Next row (rs): Pick up and k2 sts previously cast on at base of first finger, k6, turn.

Next row: Cast on 1 st, p this st, p14, turn (15 sts).

Next row: Cast on 1 st, k this st, k15 (16 sts).

Beginning with a p row, work another 25 rows in stockinette stitch on these 16 sts only, ending with rs facing.

Break off yarn, making sure you leave enough to sew the seam, and thread the yarn through the sts. Pull up tight and fasten securely. Backstitch the finger seam.

Shaping third finger

With rs facing, rejoin yarn to rem sts.

Next row (rs): Pick up and k2 sts previously cast on at base of second finger, k5, turn.

Next row: Cast on 1 st, p this st, p12, turn (13 sts).

Next row: Cast on 1 st, k this st, k13 (14 sts).

Beginning with a p row, work another 21 rows in stockinette stitch on these 14 sts only, ending with rs facing.

Break off yarn, making sure you leave enough to sew the seam, and thread the yarn through the sts. Pull up tight and fasten securely. Backstitch the finger seam.

Shaping fourth finger

With rs facing, rejoin yarn to rem sts.

Next row (rs): Pick up and k2 sts previously cast on at base of third finger, k to end.

Beginning with a p row, work another 17 rows in stockinette stitch on these 12 sts only, ending with rs facing.

Break off yarn, making sure you leave enough to sew the remaining finger and side seam, and thread the yarn through the sts. Pull up tight and fasten securely.

Finishing

Before sewing the side seams, use yarn C to embroider darts of Swiss darning on the gloves, working from the wrist area out toward each finger and thumb. Use the photograph on page 95 for guidance on where to position the darts or create your own design. Press on the wrong side, weave in the ends, and backstitch the side seams.

New skills: swiss darning

Sometimes referred to as duplicate stitch, Swiss darning is a good way of adding small areas of color after knitting a project. Take care to use a yarn similar in weight to the knitted fabric you are working with so that the stitch underneath is covered completely. Here, the darning yarn is doubled to cover the thicker main yarn.

1 Insert the needle from the back of the work to the front through the base of the stitch to be covered. Pass the needle underneath both loops of the stitch above.

2 Take the needle from front to back through the base of the original stitch (where it first came out), covering 1 stitch.

3 Bring the yarn through the base of the next stitch to be worked and continue.

Project 21: Beaded pompon hat

This delicately colored hat with subtle beading is topped with a pair of pompons, making it both fun to make and pretty to wear. The hat is fully fashioned to create the squared crown and round sides.

before you start

Measurements	One size to fit average-sized woman's head
Materials	2oz (50g) balls (approx. 200yds/183m per ball) sportweight merino yarn in 2 colors: **Yarn A** Pale blue x 1 ball **Yarn B** Pale green x 1 ball 105 small clear beads
Needles	1 pair size 2 (2.75mm) needles 1 pair size 3 (3.25mm) needles
Gauge	28 sts x 36 rows to 4in (10cm) measured over stockinette stitch using size 3 (3.25mm) needles
Abbreviations	b1—place 1 bead; beg—beginning; foll—following; inc 1—increasing 1 stitch by knitting into front and back of next stitch; k—knit; k2tog—knit 2 stitches together; m2—make 2 stitches by picking up horizontal bar before next stitch, putting it onto left needle, then knitting into back and front of it; p—purl; rs—right side; st(s)—stitch(es); tbl—through back of loop

New skills

Adding beads, see page 41

Knitting the hat
Thread the beads onto yarn A. Using size 2 (2.75mm) needles and yarn B, cast on 134 sts.
Row 1 (rs): P2, (k2, p2) to end.
Row 2: K2, (p2, k2) to end.
Without breaking off yarn B, join yarn A.
Rows 3–4: Using yarn A, repeat rows 1 and 2.
Rows 5–6: Using yarn B, repeat rows 1 and 2, inc 1 at beg and end of row 6 (136 sts).
Break off yarn B. Change to size 3 (3.25mm) needles and continue working in yarn A only.
Rows 7–12: Beginning with a k row, work 6 rows in stockinette stitch.
Row 13: K110, (b1, k1) 11 times, k to end.
Rows 14–16: Beginning with a p row, work 3 rows in stockinette stitch.
Row 17: K28, (b1, k1) 16 times, k to end.
Rows 18–24: Beginning with a p row, work 7 rows in stockinette stitch.
Row 25: K81, (b1, k1) 10 times, k to end.
Rows 26–28: Beginning with a p row, work 3 rows in stockinette stitch.
Row 29: K5, (b1, k1) 6 times, k to end.
Rows 30–32: Beginning with a p row, work 3 rows in stockinette stitch.
Row 33: K122, (b1, k1) 6 times, k to end.
Row 34: P all sts.
Row 35: K41, (b1, k1) 12 times, k to end.
Rows 36–40: Beginning with a p row, work 5 rows in stockinette stitch.
Row 41: K70, (b1, k1) 9 times, k to end.
Rows 42–46: Beginning with a p row, work 5 rows in stockinette stitch.
Row 47: K92, (b1, k1) 11 times, k to end.
Row 48: P all sts.
Row 49: K13, (b1, k1) 8 times, k to end.
Row 50: P all sts.

Shaping the crown
Row 51: (K2tog tbl, k30, k2tog) 4 times (128 sts).
Rows 52–54: Beginning with a p row, work 3 rows in stockinette stitch.
Row 55: K2tog tbl, k28, k2tog, k2tog tbl, k9, (b1, k1) 6 times, k7, k2tog, (k2tog tbl, k28, k2tog) twice (120 sts).
Rows 56–58: Beginning with a p row, work 3 rows in stockinette stitch.

Row 59: (K2tog tbl, k26, k2tog) 3 times, k2tog tbl, k13, (b1, k1) 5 times, k3, k2tog (112 sts).
Rows 60–62: Beginning with a p row, work 3 rows in stockinette stitch.
Row 63: (K2tog tbl, k24, k2tog) 4 times (104 sts).
Row 64: P all sts.
Row 65: (K2tog tbl, k22, k2tog) 4 times (96 sts).
Row 66: P all sts.
Row 67: (K2tog tbl, k20, k2tog) 4 times (88 sts).
Row 68: P all sts.

Row 69: K46, (b1, k1) 5 times, k to end.
Rows 70–72: Beginning with a p row, work 3 rows in stockinette stitch.
Row 73: (K22, m2, k22) twice (92 sts).
Row 74: P all sts.
Row 75: (K23, m2, k23) twice (96 sts).
Row 76: P all sts.
Row 77: (K24, m2, k24) twice (100 sts).
Rows 78–80: Beginning with a p row, work 3 rows in stockinette stitch. Break off yarn A.
Row 81: Using yarn B, k all sts.
Bind off purlwise.

Finishing

Weave in the ends and backstitch the side seam very neatly. Turn the hat right side out and position the seam at center back. Overcast the top seam using yarn B. Make two 1¼in (3cm) diameter pompons using yarn B, leaving 6in (15cm) tails of yarn to attach them to the corners of the hat.

New skills:
making pompons

Pompons are very easy to make using a pompon maker or circles of cardboard.
1 Cut out 2 circles of cardboard about 1in (2.5cm) larger than the pompon you want to make. Cut a small wedge out of each circle, then cut out a central 1in (2.5cm) hole.
2 Holding the circles together and starting at the outer edge, wind the yarn around the circles until they are completely covered and the central hole is almost full. Cut the yarn. If you are using a pompon maker and the central hole is too small to push the yarn through, thread a large yarn needle with as many ends of yarn as it will take; the yarn ends should be about 3ft (1m) long. Use the needle to thread the yarn through the center of the pompon maker.
3 Push the blade of a pair of scissors between the 2 disks and cut around the pompon.
4 Tie a piece of yarn around the center of the pompon as tightly as possible. Remove the disks and trim the pompon to form a neat ball.

1
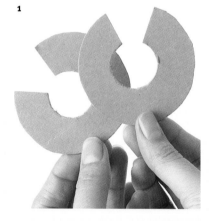

3

2

4

If you like pompons, why not make the matching beaded pompon scarf to go with this hat (see page 54)?

Project 22: Zigzag poncho

Made up of two rectangles, this poncho combines an Aran-weight cotton/acrylic mix yarn with an open mesh texture, allowing you to get to grips with a lace effect that is quick to knit and light to wear. The garter stitch edges are an easy way to create a finished look for the V-neck.

before you start

Measurements
One size to fit average-sized woman

Materials
8 x 2oz (50g) balls (approx. 98yds/90m per ball) Aran-weight cotton/acrylic mix yarn

Needles
1 pair size 9 (5.5mm) needles

Gauge
14 sts x 24 rows to 4in (10cm) measured over pattern using size 9 (5.5mm) needles

Abbreviations
k—knit; k5w—knit next 5 stitches wrapping yarn twice around needle for each stitch; p—purl; patt—pattern; rep—repeat; rs—right side; st(s)—stitch(es); ws—wrong side

Knitting the poncho
RECTANGLES (MAKE 2)
Using size 9 (5.5mm) needles, cast on 73 sts.
Rows 1–4: K all sts.

Zigzag pattern
Row 5 (rs): K9, *k5w, k6, rep from * to last 9 sts, k to end.
Row 6: K3, p12, *k5 dropping extra loops, p6, rep from * to last 3 sts, k3.
Row 7: K10, *k5w, k6, rep from * to last 8 sts, k to end.
Row 8: K3, p11, k5 dropping extra loops, *p6, k5 dropping extra loops, rep from * to last 10 sts, p7, k3.
Row 9: K11, *k5w, k6, rep from * to last 7 sts, k to end.
Row 10: K3, p10, k5 dropping extra loops, *p6, k5 dropping extra loops, rep from * to last 11 sts, p8, k3.
Row 11: K12, *k5w, k6, rep from * to last 6 sts, k to end.
Row 12: K3, p9, k5 dropping extra loops, *p6, k5 dropping extra loops, rep from * to last 12 sts, p9, k3.
Row 13: K13, *k5w, k6, rep from * to last 5 sts, k to end.
Row 14: K3, p8, k5 dropping extra loops, *p6, k5 dropping extra loops, rep from * to last 13 sts, p10, k3.
Row 15: K14, *k5w, k6, rep from * to last 4 sts, k to end.
Row 16: K3, p7, k5 dropping extra loops, *p6, k5 dropping extra loops, rep from * to last 14 sts, p11, k3.

Row 17: K15, *k5w, k6, rep from * to last 3 sts, k to end.
Row 18: K3, p6, k5 dropping extra loops, *p6, k5 dropping extra loops, rep from * to last 15 sts, p12, k3.
Row 19: Repeat row 15.
Row 20: Repeat row 16.
Row 21: Repeat row 13.
Row 22: Repeat row 14.
Row 23: Repeat row 11.
Row 24: Repeat row 12.
Row 25: Repeat row 9.
Row 26: Repeat row 10.
Row 27: Repeat row 7.
Row 28: Repeat row 8.
Row 29: Repeat row 5.
Row 30: Repeat row 6.
Work in patt as established by rows 5–30 until 6 more repeats have been completed.
Next row: K all sts.
Bind off knitwise.

Finishing
Weave in the ends and press both pieces. Measure 20½in (52cm) up the left side of each rectangle and place a marker. With right sides facing, overcast the bind-off edge of the first rectangle along the left side of the second rectangle, beginning at the cast-on edge of the second rectangle and ending at the marker. Repeat for the other seam. Press both seams on the wrong side.

The zigzag pattern provides plenty of textural detail on this poncho, but you could add fringing around the base if you wish (see page 66).

Project 23: Cute casual bag

Ideal for casual evenings or chic lunch dates, this stylish bag may look complicated but is actually easy to make. It works best when knitted in plain-colored bulky yarn to show up the lacy stitch definition to its best advantage.

before you start

Measurements	11in (28cm) wide x 12in (30cm) long
Materials	4 x 2oz (50g) balls (approx. 69yds/63m per ball) bulky-weight extra fine merino yarn
Needles	3 size 8 (5mm) needles
Gauge	17 sts x 22 rows to 4in (10cm) measured over stockinette stitch using size 8 (5mm) needles
Abbreviations	k—knit; k2tog/k3tog—knit 2 or 3 stitches together; p—purl; p2tog/p3tog—purl 2 or 3 stitches together; rs—right side; skpo—slip 1 stitch from left to right needle without working it, knit 1 stitch, pass slipped stitch over knitted stitch; sl—slip 1 stitch knitwise from left to right needle without working; st(s)—stitch(es); ws—wrong side; yf—bring yarn forward between needles

Knitting the bag

Bag panels (make 2)

Using size 8 (5mm) needles, cast on 45 sts.

Rows 1–2: P all sts.

Row 3 (rs): P1, p2tog, p5, yf, (k1, yf, p5, p3tog, p5, yf) twice, k1, yf, p5, p2tog, p1.

Row 4: P all sts.

Rows 5–14: Repeat rows 3 and 4 five times.

Row 15: P1, p2tog, p3, yf, k2tog, yf, (k1, yf, skpo, yf, p3, p3tog, p3, yf, k2tog, yf) twice, k1, yf, skpo, yf, p3, p2tog, p1.

Row 16 and all ws rows: K1, p to last st, k1.

Row 17: P1, p2tog, p2, yf, k2tog, k1, yf, (k1, yf, k1, skpo, yf, p2, p3tog, p2, yf, k2tog, k1, yf) twice, k1, yf, k1, skpo, yf, p2, p2tog, p1.

Row 19: P1, p2tog, p1, yf, k2tog, k2, yf, (k1, yf, k2, skpo, yf, p1, p3tog, p1, yf, k2tog, k2, yf) twice, k1, yf, k2, skpo, yf, p1, p2tog, p1.

Row 21: P1, p2tog, yf, k2tog, k3, yf, (k1, yf, k3, skpo, yf, p3tog, yf, k2tog, k3, yf) twice, k1, yf, k3, skpo, yf, p2tog, p1.

Row 23: P1, p2tog, yf, skpo, k3, yf, (k1, yf, k3, k2tog, yf, p3tog, yf, skpo, k3, yf) twice, k1, yf, k3, k2tog, yf, p2tog, p1.

Rows 25 & 27: Repeat row 23.

Row 29: P1, k2, yf, skpo, k3, (k4, k2tog, yf, k3, yf, skpo, k3) twice, k4, k2tog, yf, k2, p1.

Rows 31 & 33: Repeat row 29.

Row 35: P1, k3, yf, skpo, k2, (k3, k2tog, yf, k5, yf, skpo, k2) twice, k3, k2tog, yf, k3, p1.

Rows 37 & 39: Repeat row 35.

Row 41: P1, k4, yf, skpo, k1, (k2, k2tog, yf, k7, yf, skpo, k1) twice, k2, k2tog, yf, k4, p1.

Row 43: Repeat row 41.

Row 45: P1, k5, yf, skpo, (k1, k2tog, yf, k9, yf, skpo) twice, k1, k2tog, yf, k5, p1.

Row 47: P1, k6, yf, (k3tog, yf, k11, yf) twice, k3tog, yf, k6, p1.

Row 49: P1, k to last st, p1.

Row 50: K1, p to last st, k1.

Rows 51–62: Repeat rows 49 and 50 six times.

Rows 63–66: P all sts.

Transfer sts to a spare needle. Make the second panel. With ws of both panels facing, use a third needle to bind off both sets of sts together knitwise.

Strap

Using size 8 (5mm) needles, cast on 7 sts.

Row 1: Sl 1, k5, sl 1.

Row 2: K all sts.

Repeat rows 1 and 2 until strap is approximately 46in (117cm) long when slightly stretched.

Finishing

Weave in the ends and sew the side seams using backstitch. Position the ends of the strap about 2½in (6cm) below the cast-on edge and sew in place, sewing one end of the strap to the back panel and the other end to the front panel.

This chunky, low-slung, easy-to-knit bag in a neutral color will go with any outfit.

Project 24: Striped beanie

This hat is worked in a very simple two-color stripe, with seed stitch accent stripes for added interest. It is very easy to knit, with simple shaping, and is a good introduction to working with multiple yarns if color work is new to you.

before you start

Measurements

One size to fit average-sized woman's head

Materials

2oz (50g) balls (approx. 123yds/113m per ball) DK merino/cotton mix yarn in 3 colors:

Yarn A   Orange x 1 ball

Yarn B   Maroon x 1 ball

Yarn C   Crimson x 1 ball

Needles

1 pair size 3 (3mm) needles

1 pair size 5 (3.75mm) needles

Gauge

24 sts x 30 rows over 4in (10cm) measured over stockinette stitch using size 5 (3.75mm) needles

Abbreviations

k—knit; k2tog—knit 2 stitches together; p—purl; rem—remaining; rep—repeat; rs—right side; st(s)—stitch(es); tbl—through back of loop

Knitting the hat

Using size 3 (3mm) needles and yarn A, cast on 112 sts, then break off yarn.

Rows 1–2: Using yarn B, (k1, p1) to end.

Rows 3–4: Using yarn C, (k1, p1) to end. Change to size 5 (3.75mm) needles.

Row 5 (rs): Using yarn B, k all sts.

Row 6: Using yarn B, p all sts.

Row 7: Using yarn C, k all sts.

Row 8: Using yarn C, p all sts.

Rows 9–12: Repeat rows 5–8.

Rows 13–14: Repeat rows 5 and 6.

Row 15: Using yarn C, k all sts.

Row 16: Using yarn A, (k1, p1) to end.

Row 17: Using yarn A, (p1, k1) to end.

Row 18: Using yarn C, p all sts.

Rows 19–36: Repeat rows 5–18 once, then repeat rows 5–8 once.

Rows 37–38: Repeat rows 5 and 6.

Row 39: Using yarn C, k all sts.

Row 40: Using yarn A, (k1, p1) to end.

Shaping the crown

Row 41 (rs): Using yarn A, *k2tog tbl, (p1, k1) 12 times, k2tog, rep from * to end (104 sts).

Row 42: Using yarn C, p all sts.

Rows 43–44: Repeat rows 5 and 6.

Row 45: Using yarn C, *k2tog tbl, k22, k2tog, rep from * to end (96 sts).

Row 46: Using yarn C, p all sts.

Row 47: Using yarn B, k2tog tbl, k20, k2tog, rep from * to end (88 sts).

Row 48: Using yarn B, p all sts.

Row 49: Using yarn C, *k2tog tbl, k18, k2tog, rep from * to end (80 sts).

Row 50: Using yarn C, p all sts.

Row 51: Using yarn B, *k2tog tbl, k16, k2tog, rep from * to end (72 sts).

Row 52: Using yarn B, *p2tog, p14, p2tog tbl, rep from * to end (64 sts).

Row 53: Using yarn C, *k2tog tbl, k12, k2tog, rep from * to end (56 sts). Break off yarns B and C and continue using yarn A only.

Row 54: *K2tog, (k1, p1) 5 times, k2tog tbl, rep from * to end (48 sts).

Row 55: *K2tog tbl, (k1, p1) 4 times, k2tog, rep from * to end (40 sts).

Row 56: (P2tog, p6, p2tog tbl) 4 times (32 sts).

Thread the end of the yarn through rem sts, pull up tight, and fasten securely.

Finishing

Weave in the ends and steam gently on the wrong side. Backstitch the back seam very neatly using yarn B.

TIP: WORKING WITH MULTIPLE YARNS

This hat is worked throughout in 2-row stripes of 3 different colors. Do not break off the yarns at the end of each stripe. Instead, carry them up the side of the work. This helps to reduce the number of ends to be woven in when finished.

Knitting stripes is the easiest way to introduce multiple colors to your accessories.

Project 25: Beaded denim bag

Knitted in indigo-dyed denim yarn, the intense beading on the strap and more restrained beaded pinstripe on the main body of the bag give it added "bling." Although knitted in one piece, the pattern is broken down into sections to make it easier to see which piece you are knitting.

before you start

Measurements

9½in (24cm) wide x 2in (5cm) deep x 5½in (14cm) high

Materials

3 x 2oz (50g) balls (approx. 102yds/93m per ball) DK denim-effect cotton yarn

800 large clear beads

1 button

Needles

1 pair size 3 (3.25mm) needles

Gauge

Before washing—23 sts x 35 rows to 4in (10cm) measured over beaded pattern used for strap

After washing—23 sts x 40 rows to 4in (10cm) measured over beaded pattern used for strap

Abbreviations

b1—place 1 bead; inc 1—increase 1 stitch by knitting into front and back of next stitch; k—knit; k2tog—knit 2 stitches together; p—purl; patt—pattern; rep—repeat; rs—right side; st(s)—stitch(es); ws—wrong side

Knitting the bag

Divide the beads into 3 roughly equal piles and thread each pile onto a separate ball of yarn. Using size 3 (3.25mm) needles, cast on 56 sts.

Front panel

Row 1 (rs): K into back of each st.

Row 2: K1, p2, *k1, p3, k1, p4, rep from * to last 8 sts, k1, p3, k1, p2, k1.

Row 3: K5, b1, *k8, b1, rep from * to last 5 sts, k5.

Row 4: K1, p2, *k1, p3, k1, p4, rep from * to last 8 sts, k1, p3, k1, p2, k1.

Rows 5–56: Repeat rows 3 and 4 twenty-four times.

Base panel

Row 57 (fold line): P all sts.

Row 58: Repeat row 2.

Rows 59–78: Repeat rows 3 and 4 ten times.

Row 79 (fold line): P all sts.

Back and top panels

Rows 80–157: Repeat rows 2–79.

Front flap

Row 158: K1, p2, *k1, p3, k1, p4, rep from * to last 8 sts, k1, p3, k1, p2, k1.

New skills

Adding beads, see page 41

Row 159: K5, b1, *k8, b1, rep from * to last 5 sts, k5.

Row 160: K1, p2, *k1, p3, k1, p4, rep from * to last 8 sts, k1, p3, k1, p2, k1.

Rows 161–172: Repeat rows 159 and 160 six times.

Shaping the flap

Note: Stitch on right needle after bind-off is not included in remaining instructions for each row; work each bind-off knitwise.

Row 173: Bind off 2 sts, k2, *b1, k8, rep from * to last 6 sts, b1, k5 (54 sts).

Row 174: Bind off 2 sts, *k1, p3, k1, p4, rep from * to last 6 sts, k1, p3, k2 (52 sts).

Row 175: Bind off 2 sts, *b1, k8, rep from * to last 4 sts, b1, k3 (50 sts).

Row 176: Bind off 2 sts, p2, *k1, p4, k1, p3, rep from * to last 9 sts, k1, p4, k1, p2, k1 (48 sts).

Row 177: Bind off 2 sts, k7, *b1, k8, rep from * to last 2 sts, k2 (46 sts).

Row 178: Bind off 2 sts, *k1, p4, k1, p3, rep from * to last 7 sts, k1, p4, k2 (44 sts).

Row 179: Bind off 2 sts, k5, *b1, k8, rep from * to end (42 sts).

Row 180: Bind off 2 sts, (p3, k1) twice, *p4, k1, p3, k1, rep from * to last 4 sts, p3, k1 (40 sts).

Row 181: Bind off 2 sts, k3, *b1, k8, rep from * to last 7 sts, b1, k6 (38 sts).

Row 182: Bind off 2 sts, p1, *k1, p3, k1, p4, rep from * to last 7 sts, k1, p3, k1, p1, k1 (36 sts).

Row 183: Bind off 2 sts, k1, *b1, k8, rep from * to last 5 sts, b1, k4 (34 sts).

TIP: TESTING FOR SHRINKAGE

This yarn is designed to shrink in length and fade in appearance like jeans. This shrinkage has been allowed for in the pattern. Take time to knit a test swatch and wash it according to the instructions on the ball band of the yarn in order to match the post-wash gauge stated in the pattern.

Row 184: Bind off 2 sts, *p3, k1, p4, k1, rep from * to last 4 sts, p3, k1 (32 sts).
Row 185: Bind off 2 sts, (k8, b1) twice, k11 (30 sts).
Row 186: Bind off 2 sts, p1, (k1, p4, k1, p3) twice, k1, p4, k1, p1, k1 (28 sts).
Row 187: Bind off 2 sts, k6, b1, k8, b1, k9 (26 sts).
Row 188: Bind off 2 sts, (p4, k1, p3, k1) twice, p4, k1 (24 sts).
Row 189: Bind off 2 sts, k4, b1, k8, b1, k7 (22 sts).
Row 190: Bind off 2 sts, p2, k1, p3, k1, p4, k1, p3, k1, p2, k1 (20 sts).
Row 191: Bind off 2 sts, k2, b1, k8, b1, k5 (18 sts).
Row 192: Bind off 2 sts, (p4, k1) 3 times (16 sts).
Row 193: Bind off 2 sts, b1, k8, b1, k3 (14 sts).
Row 194: Bind off 2 sts, p2, k1, p4, k1, p2, k1 (12 sts).
Row 195: Bind off 2 sts, k to end (10 sts).
Row 196: Bind off 2 sts, k1, p4, k2 (8 sts). Bind off knitwise.

Strap

Using size 3 (3.25mm) needles, cast on 13 sts.
Row 1 (rs): K into back of each st.
Row 2 and all ws rows: K2, p to last 2 sts, k2.
Row 3: K3, *b1, k1, rep from * to last 2 sts, k2.
Row 5: K all sts.

Row 7: K2, *b1, k1, rep from * to last st, k1.
Row 9: K all sts.
Rows 10–64: Continue patt as established by rows 2–9, ending with rs facing for next row.
Row 65: K2tog, k to last 2 sts, k2tog (11 sts).
Rows 66–112: Continue patt as established by rows 2–9, ending with rs facing for next row.
Row 113: K2tog, k to last 2 sts, k2tog (9 sts).
Rows 114–192: Continue patt as established by rows 2–9, ending with rs facing for next row.
Row 193: K2, inc 1, k to last 3 sts, inc 1, k2 (11 sts).

Rows 194–240: Continue patt as established by rows 2–9, ending with rs facing for next row.
Row 241: K2, inc 1, k to last 3 sts, inc 1, k2 (13 sts).
Rows 242–304: Continue patt as established by rows 2–9, ending with rs facing. Bind off knitwise.

Finishing

Weave in the ends. Wash the bag, strap, and enough yarn to sew the bag together. Allow to dry, then press the bag and strap on the wrong side. Place markers on each side of the strap 5½in (14cm) from the cast-on edge. With wrong sides facing, match up the cast-on edge of the strap with the base panel of the bag and pin in place. Next, match the markers on the strap to the top of the front and back panels and pin in place. Using doubled yarn, blanket stitch the seams together on the right side to create an exterior seam. Repeat for the other side of the bag. Sew a button in the center of the front panel, 4in (10cm) down from the cast-on edge. Make a button loop at the tip of the front flap. Weave in the ends.

New skills:
making a button loop

This is a very simple but sturdy way of making a loop for fastening a button.
1 Use a single end of yarn to sew a loop just big enough to pass the button through, positioning the loop between the lines of purl stitch. Make sure that the loop is secure at both ends.
2 Working from one end to the other, reinforce the loop with blanket stitch.

1

2

Project 26: Lacy beaded hat

Three different colors of beads have been used to give the floral motifs in this lacy hat more detail. The lace pattern worked into the fully fashioned shaping on the crown may look complicated, but the charted instructions make it easier to follow.

before you start

Measurements

One size to fit average-sized woman's head

Materials

1 x 2oz (50g) ball (approx. 123yds/113m per ball) DK merino/cotton mix yarn

32 large clear beads

27 large white beads

21 large mauve beads

Needles

1 pair size 5 (3.75mm) needles

Gauge

24 sts x 30 rows to 4in (10cm) measured over stockinette stitch using size 5 (3.75mm) needles

Abbreviations

inc 1—increase 1 stitch by purling into front and back of next stitch; k—knit; k2tog—knit 2 stitches together; p—purl; rs—right side; skpo—slip 1 stitch from left to right needle without working it, knit 1 stitch, pass slipped stitch over knitted stitch; st(s)—stitch(es); ws—wrong side; yf—bring yarn forward between needles

Knitting the hat

Thread the yarn with beads in the correct color sequence. Using size 5 (3.75mm) needles, cast on 100 sts. Begin working from the chart on page 110, placing the lace pattern and beaded motifs as indicated. Increase on row 6 using inc 1; specific methods of decreasing are indicated on the chart. When the last row of the chart has been completed, break off the yarn, leaving an end about 8in (20cm) long. Thread the end of the yarn through the remaining 22 sts. Pull up tight and fasten off.

Finishing

Backstitch the back seam very neatly and press gently. Do not press the ribbing.

TIP: BEADING SEQUENCE

When knitting with beads of more than one color, remember to thread them onto the yarn in the reverse order to the way you will be knitting them. Following the chart on page 110, start at the top and read down from left to right on each of the beading rows.

The beading sequence for this project is: 5 clear, 1 mauve, 1 clear, 2 mauve, 1 clear, 2 mauve, 1 clear, 13 mauve, (2 white, 1 mauve, 2 white, 2 clear) 3 times, 15 white, 18 clear

KEY

☐ K on rs, p on ws

⊡ P on rs, k on ws

◿ K2tog

◺ Skpo

⬭ Yf

▨ Stitch not in work
due to shaping

⊙ Place 1 mauve bead

⊙ Place 1 clear bead

⊡ Place 1 white bead

New skills

Adding beads, see page 41

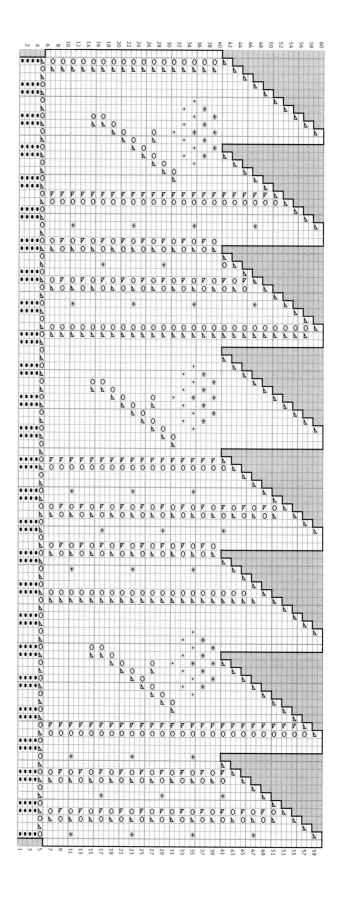

Knit this pretty
hat to go with
the matching
lacy beaded scarf
on page 66.

Project 27: Felted booties

These booties were inspired by traditional Scandinavian slippers. Each bootee comprises blocks of texture and color knitted in two pieces: one made up of six squares, the other just two. The clever way in which the pieces are folded and sewn means there is no need for shaping. The completed booties are felted to make them even softer to wear.

before you start

Measurements	One size to fit average-sized woman's feet
Materials	2oz (50g) balls (approx. 123yds/113m per ball) DK tweed-effect wool yarn in 3 colors:
	Yarn A Beige x 1 ball
	Yarn B Turquoise x 1 ball
	Yarn C Blue x 1 ball
Needles	1 pair size 9 (5.5mm) needles
Gauge	**After felting**—18 sts x 30 rows to 4in (10cm) measured over stockinette stitch using size 9 (5.5mm) needles
Abbreviations	k—knit; p—purl; rs—right side; st(s)—stitch(es)

TIP: FELTING A TEST SWATCH
Felt a test swatch as instructed for the patchwork bag (see page 62).

Knitting the booties
PIECE 1 (MAKE 2)

Using size 9 (5.5mm) needles and yarn A, cast on 16 sts.

Square 1
Row 1 (rs): K1, (p4, k1) to end.
Row 2: K5, p1, k4, p1, k5.
Rows 3–6: Repeat rows 1 and 2 twice.
Row 7: K all sts.
Row 8: P all sts.
Rows 9–16: Repeat rows 1 and 2 four times.
Rows 17–26: Repeat rows 7–16.
Break off yarn A and join yarn B.

Square 2
Carry yarns up edge of work throughout this square.
Row 1 (rs): Using yarn B, (p1, k1) to end.
Row 2: Using yarn B, k all sts.
Rows 3–4: Using yarn C, repeat rows 1 and 2.
Rows 5–24: Repeat rows 1–4 five times.
Rows 25–26: Using yarn C, repeat rows 1 and 2. Break off yarn C.

Square 3
Row 1 (rs): Using yarn B, k1, p1, k5, p2, k5, p1, k1.
Row 2: (K2, p5) twice, k2.
Row 3: K2, (p1, k3, p1, k2) twice.
Row 4: K1, p1, k1, p3, k1, p2, k1, p3, k1, p1, k1.
Row 5: K3, p1, k1, p1, k4, p1, k1, p1, k3.
Row 6: K1, p2, k1, p1, k1, p4, k1, p1, k1, p2, k1.
Row 7: K4, p1, k6, p1, k4.
Row 8: K1, p3, k1, p6, k1, p3, k1.
Row 9: Repeat row 5.
Row 10: Repeat row 6.
Row 11: Repeat row 3.
Row 12: Repeat row 4.
Rows 13–24: Repeat rows 1–12.
Rows 25–26: Repeat rows 1 and 2. Break off yarn B.

Square 4
Carry yarns up edge of work throughout this square.
Row 1 (rs): Using yarn C, (p1, k1) to end.
Row 2: Using yarn C, k all sts.
Row 3: Using yarn A, (p1, k1) to end.
Row 4: Using yarn A, k all sts.

These felted Scandinavian-style booties make perfect slippers. They're so soft and comfy, you won't ever want to take them off.

Row 5: Using yarn B, k1, p to last st, k1.

Row 6: Using yarn C, k all sts.

Rows 7–24: Repeat rows 1–6 three times.

Rows 25–26: Using yarn C, repeat rows 1 and 2. Break off yarns A and B.

Square 5

Row 1 (rs): Using yarn C, (k2, p5) twice, k2.

Row 2: K1, p1, k5, p2, k5, p1, k1.

Row 3: K1, p1, k1, p3, k1, p2, k1, p3, k1, p1, k1.

Row 4: K2, (p1, k3, p1, k2) twice.

Row 5: K1, p2, k1, p1, k1, p4, k1, p1, k1, p2, k1.

Row 6: K3, p1, k1, p1, k4, p1, k1, p1, k3.

Row 7: K1, p3, k1, p6, k1, p3, k1.

Row 8: K4, p1, k6, p1, k4.

Row 9: K1, p2, k1, p1, k1, p4, k1, p1, k1, p2, k1.

Row 10: K3, p1, k1, p1, k4, p1, k1, p1, k3.

Row 11: K1, p1, k1, p3, k1, p2, k1, p3, k1, p1, k1.

Row 12: K2, (p1, k3, p1, k2) twice.

Rows 13–24: Repeat rows 1–12.

Rows 25–26: Repeat rows 1 and 2. Break off yarn C.

Square 6

Carry yarns up edge of work throughout this square.

Row 1 (rs): Using yarn A, k1, p to last st, k1.

Row 2: Using yarn A, k all sts.

Row 3: Using yarn B, k1, p to last st, k1.

Row 4: Using yarn B, k all sts.

Rows 5–24: Repeat rows 1–4 five times.

Rows 25–26: Using yarn B, k all sts. Bind off knitwise.

PIECE 2 (MAKE 2)

Using size 9 (5.5mm) needles and yarn C, cast on 16 sts.

Square 1

Carry yarns up edge of work throughout this square.

Row 1 (rs): Using yarn C, k1, p to last st, k1.

Row 2: Using yarn C, k all sts.

Row 3: Using yarn A, k1, p to last st, k1.

Row 4: Using yarn A, k all sts.

Rows 5–24: Repeat rows 1–4 five times.

Rows 25–26: Using yarn A, repeat rows 1 and 2. Break off both yarns.

Square 2

Row 1 (rs): Using yarn B, k5, p1, k4, p1, k5.

Row 2: K1, (p4, k1) 3 times.

Rows 3–6: Repeat rows 1 and 2 twice.

Row 7: P all sts.

Row 8: K all sts.

Rows 9–16: Repeat rows 1 and 2 four times.

Row 17: P all sts.

Row 18: K all sts.

Rows 19–24: Repeat rows 1 and 2 three times.

Rows 25–26: K all sts. Bind off knitwise.

Finishing

Weave in the ends. With right sides facing, join the 2 pieces of each bootee. Follow the diagrams for assembling the booties, folding where indicated and backstitching matching colored edges together. Turn right side out, felt, and allow to dry. Using yarn C, finish the opening edges with blanket stitch. Make a 1¼in (3cm) long tassel using yarn A and sew in place at the base of the front opening.

New skills: making tassels

The tassels used to embellish these booties are very easy to make.

1 Wrap some yarn around a piece of cardboard that is the length of the tassel you want to make. Around 10 wraps are used here.

2 Thread a piece of yarn C through the top of the tassel between the yarn and the cardboard, tie to secure, and leave a long end for sewing the tassel in place later.

3 Cut the yarn along the bottom edge of the cardboard.

4 Wrap a length of yarn around the tassel near the top, knot tightly, then repeat 1 or 2 times. Trim the tassel.

1

3

2

4

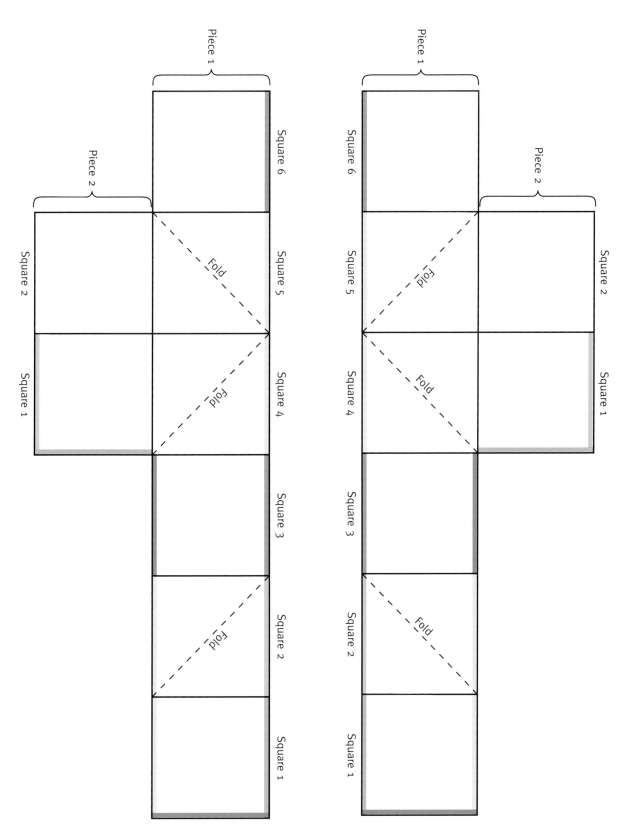

Project 28: Floral relief scarf

This colorful scarf alternates blocks of stripes with a large rotating floral motif worked in reverse stockinette stitch, creating a relief effect. The centers of the flowers are highlighted with Swiss-darned embroidery after knitting.

before you start

Measurements
9in (23cm) wide x 61½in (156cm) long

Materials
2oz (50g) balls (approx. 123yds/113m per ball) DK merino/cotton mix yarn in 4 colors:

Yarn A   Maroon x 2 balls
Yarn B   Crimson x 2 balls
Yarn C   Brown x 1 ball
Yarn D   Orange x 1 ball

Needles
1 pair size 5 (3.75mm) needles

Gauge
24 sts x 30 rows to 4in (10cm) measured over stockinette stitch using size 5 (3.75mm) needles

Abbreviations
k—knit; p—purl; rs—right side; st(s)—stitch(es); ws—wrong side

Knitting the scarf

Using size 5 (3.75mm) needles and yarn A, cast on 52 sts. Break off yarn A.

Row 1 (rs): Using yarn D, (k1, p1) to end.
Row 2: (P1, k1) to end. Break off yarn D.
Rows 3–4: Using yarn B, repeat rows 1 and 2. Break off yarn B.

Join yarn C and continue knitting the scarf from the charts on pages 117 and 118, beginning with square 1 and continuing until you have completed square 7, changing colors as indicated.

Next row: Using yarn C, repeat rows 1 and 2.
Next row: Using yarn A, repeat rows 1 and 2. Using yarn D, bind off in seed stitch.

Finishing

Weave in the ends. Place Swiss darning in the center of the flowers as indicated on the charts, using colors as follows: yarn D on square 1, yarn A on square 3, yarn D on square 5, and yarn C on square 7. Gently steam the scarf on the wrong side.

KEY

☐	K on rs, p on ws	▨	Yarn A—Maroon
⊡	P on rs, k on ws	▨	Yarn B—Crimson
♡	Swiss darn	▨	Yarn C—Brown
		▨	Yarn D—Orange

Square 1

Square 3

Squares 2 & 6

Square 4

New skills

Swiss darning, see page 96

TIP: ENLARGING CHARTS

Enlarge the charts on a photocopier to make them easier to follow and mark off each row as you go.

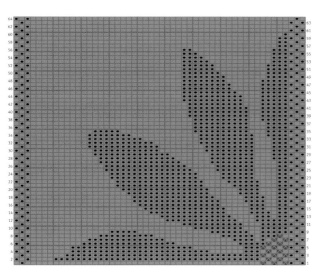

Square 5

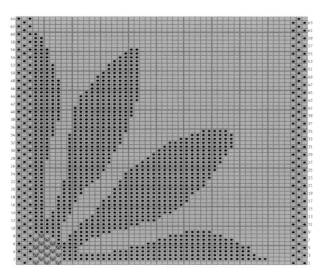

Square 7

KEY

☐ K on rs, p on ws
● P on rs, k on ws
♡ Swiss darn
▨ Yarn A—Maroon
▨ Yarn B—Crimson
▨ Yarn C—Brown
▨ Yarn D—Orange

The striped squares on the scarf coordinate with the striped beanie on page 104.

Project 29: Summer bag and coin purse

This cotton bag is knitted in summery shades and has a matching beaded coin purse that you can knit from the leftover yarn. The combination of purl stitch and ribbing together with the use of doubled yarn not only gives the bag its firm fabric, but also means it does not need to be lined.

before you start

Measurements

Bag 12in (30cm) wide x 11in (28cm) high x 3¼in (8cm) deep

Purse 4in (10cm) wide x 3¼in (8cm) long

Materials

2oz (50g) balls (approx. 125yds/115m per ball) sportweight cotton yarn in 5 colors:

Yarn A Turquoise x 5 balls   **Yarn B** Blue x 2 balls

Yarn C Yellow x 2 balls   **Yarn D** Cream x 2 balls

Yarn E Green x 2 balls

All yarns are used doubled throughout

120 small green beads

4in (10cm) lightweight cream zipper

Needles

3 size 5 (3.75mm) needles

Gauge

20 sts x 25 rows to 4in (10cm) measured over stockinette stitch using size 5 (3.75mm) needles and doubled yarn

Abbreviations

b1—place 1 bead; k—knit; p—purl; patt—pattern; rep—repeat; rs—right side; st(s)—stitch(es); ws—wrong side

Knitting the bag
Main panels (make 2)

Using size 5 (3.75mm) needles and yarn A (remember to double all the yarns), cast on 64 sts.

Row 1 (rs): K1, *p2, k3, rep from * to last 3 sts, p2, k1.

Row 2: K1, p3, k1, *p4, k1, rep from * to last 4 sts, p3, k1.

Rows 3–32: Repeat rows 1 and 2 fifteen times. Break off yarn A and join yarn C.

Row 33: P all sts.

Row 34: K all sts.

Break off yarn C and join yarn D to begin the striped pattern.

Row 35: K1, *p2, k3, rep from * to last 3 sts, p2, k1.

Row 36: K1, p to last st, k1.

Continue to work in patt as established by rows 35 and 36, carrying yarns up side of work or breaking off and joining yarns as needed to work the stripe sequence as follows:

Rows 37–38: Yarn E.

Rows 39–40: Yarn B.

Rows 41–42: Yarn A.

Rows 43–44: Yarn C.

Rows 45–46: Yarn D.

Rows 47–86: Continuing to work in patt, repeat this stripe sequence 4 times.

Rows 87–92: Continuing to work in patt, repeat rows 37–42 once, ending with rs facing. Join yarn C.

Row 93: P all sts.

Row 94: K all sts.

Using yarn C, bind off knitwise.

This summer bag is the
perfect size for carrying
everything you need for
a day out at the beach
or park. Keep your keys
and coins safe and handy
in the matching purse.

Side panels (make 2)

Using size 5 (3.75mm) needles and yarn A, cast on 17 sts.

Row 1: K1, p1, (k3, p2) twice, k3, p1, k1.

Row 2: K1, p2, (k1, p4) twice, k1, p2, k1.

Rows 3–70: Continue to work in patt as established by rows 1 and 2. Break off yarn A and join yarn C.

Row 71: P all sts.

Row 72: K all sts.

Using yarn C, bind off knitwise.

Handles (make 2)

Using size 5 (3.75mm) needles and yarn C, cast on 89 sts. Break off yarn C and join yarn A.

Row 1: K1, *p2, k3, rep from * to last 3 sts, p2, k1.

Row 2: K1, p3, k1, *p4, k1, rep from * to last 4 sts, p3, k1.

Rows 3–6: Repeat rows 1 and 2 twice. Break off yarn A and join yarn C.

Rows 7–13: Repeat rows 1 and 2 until 13 rows have been completed.

Bind off (see new skills).

Finishing

Weave in the ends and press carefully. Put the two main panels together, right sides facing and top and bottom edges matching. Sew together at the cast-on edge using backstitch. Press the seam on the wrong side. Measure 1½in (4cm) either side of this bottom seam and mark using a scrap of contrast yarn. With wrong sides of each side panel and main piece touching, match up the top edges and the bottom corners of the side panels with

TIP: USING DOUBLED YARN

If you are using a doubled length of yarn but have only one ball of color, take one end from the outside of the ball and the other from the inside.

New skills:
binding the handles

The handles need to be doubled lengthwise to make them stronger. You could overcast the edges together or use this alternative method of binding off to create a strong but decorative edge.

1 Using the right needle, lift up the first stitch of the cast-on edge and knit it together with the first stitch on the left needle through the back of the loop.

2 Repeat for each stitch across the row, folding and sealing the handle at the same time. Bind off all the stitches purlwise to complete the handle.

the markers. Using yarn A, join the seam on the right side using blanket stitch to create an exterior seam. With the yarn A side facing outward, position the handles 2⅜in (6cm) below the top edge of the bag and 2⅜in (6cm) in from the side seams. Sew in place and weave in the ends.

Knitting the purse

Thread 24 beads onto each of the five colors of yarn, remembering to use all the yarns doubled. Using size 5 (3.75mm) needles and yarn B, cast on 44 sts.

Row 1 (rs): K1, *p2, k1, b1, k1, rep from * to last 3 sts, p2, k1.

Row 2: K1, p to last st, k1.

Continue to work in patt as established by rows 1 and 2, carrying yarns up side of work or breaking off and joining yarns as needed to work the stripe sequence as follows:

Rows 3–4: Yarn A.

Rows 5–6: Yarn C.

Rows 7–8: Yarn D.

Rows 9–10: Yarn E.

Rows 11–30: Repeat rows 1–10 twice.

Row 31: Using yarn E, k22, turn so that wrong sides are together, and use a third needle to bind off both sets of sts together knitwise.

Finishing

Weave in the ends and press on the wrong side. Backstitch the side seam. Position the zipper in the cast-on edge opening and overcast into place using a sewing needle and thread.

New skills

Adding beads, see page 41

Project 30: Dimple stitch shawl

This openwork lace pattern is formed over four rows, with the decreasing worked into the pattern. The cast-on edge is the widest point, so you may find it easier to cast on using a long circular needle and change to straight needles as the shawl narrows.

before you start

Measurements
82¾in (210cm) at widest point x
47¼in (120cm) long

Materials
6 x 2oz (50g) balls (approx.
197yds/180m per ball) DK merino/
alpaca mix tweed-effect yarn

Needles
1 pair size 9 (5.5mm) needles
3ft (1m) size 9 (5.5mm) circular
needle (optional)

Gauge
17 sts x 19 rows to 4in (10cm)
measured over pattern using size 9
(5.5mm) needles

Abbreviations
k—knit; k4tog—knit 4 stitches
together; p—purl; p2tog/p3tog—
purl 2 or 3 stitches together;
rep—repeat; rs—right side;
sl 4—refer to step-by-step
instructions on page 124;
st(s)—stitch(es); tbl—through
back of loop; ws—wrong side;
y2rn—wrap yarn twice around
needle; yb—take yarn back
between needles; yf—bring yarn
forward between needles

Knitting the shawl
Using size 9 (5.5mm) needles, cast on
334 sts.
Rows 1–3: P all sts.
Row 4 (ws): P1, *y2rn, p1, rep from * to
last st, p1.
Row 5 (rs): P1, yb, *sl 4, (yf, k4tog tbl)
twice in same 4 sts, rep from * to last
st, p1.
Rows 6–7: (P2tog) twice, p to last 4 sts,
(p2tog) twice.
Continue in pattern as established by rows
4–7 until 6 sts remain.

Last pattern repeat
Next row: P1, (y2rn, p1) 4 times, p1.
Next row: P1, yb, sl 4, (yf, k4tog tbl) twice
in same 4 sts, p1 (6 sts).
Next row: P all sts.
Next row: (P2tog) 3 times (3 sts).
Next row: P3tog and finish off.

Finishing
Weave in the ends. Block and pin the
shawl to its finished size and press lightly
on the wrong side, taking care not to
flatten the texture.

TIP: USING MARKERS
Slip markers made from scraps of
yarn onto the needle about every
20 stitches to keep track of the
number of stitches you are casting on.

New skills: dimple stitch

The lace pattern of this shawl may look intricate but it is actually very easy to work.

1 Work as instructed for row 4, wrapping the yarn twice around the right needle in a counterclockwise direction where indicated.

2 On the next row, take the yarn to the back of the knitting where indicated and slip the next 4 stitches purlwise onto the right needle without working them. As you do so, drop the extra loops that you created in the previous row when you wrapped the yarn twice around the needle.

3 Slip the 4 stitches back onto the left needle.

4 Bring the yarn forward to the front of the work again and knit the 4 stitches together through the backs of the loops, leaving the 4 stitches on the left needle.

5 Repeat step 4, but this time take the 4 stitches off the left needle when you have worked them. You have now made 4 stitches to replace 4 stitches. Continue working the row.

2

3

4

1

5

This shawl is light to wear but will keep out the chill on crisp spring and fall days. Wear it for country walks or when snuggling up in front of a fire—its beautifully delicate design will always give you pleasure.

Yarns and suppliers

Below is a list of the specific yarns used to make the projects. If you cannot find any of these yarns, or simply wish to make an accessory in a different yarn, use the information supplied here to help you choose a suitable alternative. Refer also to the beginning of each project, where you will find the quantity, weight, and fiber content of the yarns used to make each accessory.

PROJECT 1, CHUNKY RIBBED SCARF
Yarn: Jaeger Chamonix; color & code: Biarritz 904; needles: 10½–11 (7mm); gauge: 14½ sts x 20 rows.

PROJECT 2, BRIGHT BEADED MITTENS
Yarn: Rowan Wool Cotton; colors & codes: A = Coffee Rich 956, B = Lavish 957, C = Spark 947, D = Gypsy 910; needles: 5–6 (3.75–4mm); gauge: 22–24 sts x 30–32 rows.

PROJECT 3, SHAGGY CHENILLE WRAP
Yarn A: Rowan Plaid; color & code: Crushed Shell 160; needles: 11 (8mm); gauge: 11–12 sts x 14–16 rows. Yarn B: Rowan Chunky Cotton Chenille; color & code: Parchment 383; needles: 7–8 (4.5–5mm); gauge: 16–18 sts x 23–25 rows.

PROJECT 4, FURRY BAG
Yarn A: Jaeger Natural Fleece; color & code: Damask 527; needles: 13 (9mm); gauge: 10½ sts x 15 rows. Yarn B: Jaeger Fur; color & code: Fox 054; needles: 15 (10mm); gauge: 8 sts x 9 rows.

PROJECT 5, SILKY SOCKS
Beaded socks
Yarn: Jaeger Silk 4 ply; color & code: Brilliant 144; needles: 2–3 (3mm); gauge: 28 sts x 38 rows.

Embroidered socks
Yarn: Jaeger Cashmina; color & code: Tea Rose 040; needles: 3 (3.25mm); gauge: 28 sts x 38 rows.

PROJECT 6, COZY CASHMERE HAT
Yarn: Jaeger Cashair; color & code: Llama 076; needles: 11 (8mm); gauge: 12 sts x 16 rows.

PROJECT 7, BEADED POMPON SCARF
Yarn: Jaeger Matchmaker Merino 4 ply; colors & codes: A = Cloud 744, B = Croquet 735; needles: 3 (3.25mm); gauge: 28 sts x 36 rows.

PROJECT 8, CLASSIC-STYLE GLOVES
Yarn: Jaeger Baby Merino 4 ply; colors & codes: main = Red Cheek 094, contrast = Marigold 096; needles: 3 (3.25mm); gauge: 28 sts x 36 rows.

PROJECT 9, LEGWARMERS
Yarn: Jaeger Extra Fine Merino Aran; colors & codes: A = Juniper 550, B = Columbian 553; needles: 7 (4.5mm); gauge: 19 sts x 25 rows.

PROJECT 10, PATCHWORK BAG
Yarn: Rowan Yorkshire Tweed DK; colors & codes: A = Scarlet 344, B = Revel 342, C = Frolic 350, D = Lime Leaf 348, E = Frog 349, F = Skip 347; needles: 6 (4mm); gauge: 20–22 sts x 28–30 rows.

PROJECT 11, LACY BEADED SCARF
Yarn: Rowan Wool Cotton; color & code: Hiss 952; needles: 5–6 (3.75–4mm); gauge: 22–24 sts x 30–32 rows.

PROJECT 12, CHUNKY RUFFLE BEANIE
Yarn: Patons Funky Chunky; colors & codes: A = Brick 05201, B = Bracken 05206; needles: 15 (10mm); gauge: 9 sts x 12 rows.

PROJECT 13, WARM WINTER MUFF
Yarn A: Jaeger Fur; color & code: Polar 048; needles: 15 (10mm); gauge: 8 sts x 9 rows. Yarn B: Jaeger Natural Fleece; color & code: Ammonite 520; needles: 13 (9mm); gauge: 10½ sts x 15 rows.

PROJECT 14, FUNKY FINGERLESS GLOVES AND WRIST WARMERS
Buttoned gloves
Yarn: Jaeger Baby Merino DK; color & code: Yoyo 193; needles: 6 (4mm); gauge: 22 sts x 30 rows.

Striped gloves
Yarn: Jaeger Extra Fine Merino DK; colors & codes: A = Coal Dust 978, B = Jet 951, C = Flannel 942; needles: 5–6 (3.75–4mm); gauge: 22 sts x 30–32 rows.

Sequinned gloves
Yarn: Jaeger Luxury Tweed; color & code: Gold Flame 822; needles: 6 (4mm); gauge: 21–23 sts x 28–31 rows.

Wrist warmers
Yarn: Rowan Wool Cotton; colors & codes: A = Coffee Rich 956, B = Gypsy 910, C = Spark 947, D = Lavish 957; needles: 5–6 (3.75–4mm); gauge: 22–24 sts x 30–32 rows.

PROJECT 15, PRETTY FLORAL BAG
Yarn A: Anchor Magic; color code: 1410; needles: 7 (4.5mm); gauge: 18 sts x 32 rows. Yarn B: Rowan Handknit DK Cotton; color & code: Ecru 251; needles: 6–7 (4–4.5mm); gauge: 19–20 sts x 28 rows.

PROJECT 16, RIBBED EARFLAP HAT
Yarn: Jaeger Extra Fine Merino Aran; colors & codes: A = Juniper 550, B = Columbian 553; needles: 7 (4.5mm); gauge: 19 sts x 25 rows.

PROJECT 17, SLOUCHING SOCKS
Yarn: Rowan Calmer; color & code: Tinkerbell 475; needles: 8 (5mm); gauge: 21 sts x 30 rows.

PROJECT 18, CABLED MITTENS
Yarn: Jaeger Chamonix; color & code: Paris 906; needles: 10½–11 (7mm); gauge: 14½ sts x 20 rows.

PROJECT 19, RAINBOW SCARF
Yarns A, B, & C: Rowan Kid Classic; colors & codes: A = Royal 835, B = Cherish 833, C = Juicy 827; needles: 8–9 (5–5.5mm); gauge: 18–19 sts x 23–25 rows. Yarns D & E: Rowan Kidsilk Haze; colors & codes: D = Dreamboat 587, E = Jelly 597; needles: 3–8 (3.25–5mm); gauge: 18–25 sts x 23–34 rows.

PROJECT 20, DRIVING GLOVES
Yarns A & B: Rowan Yorkshire Tweed DK; colors & codes: A = Frog 349, B = Lime Leaf 348; needles: 6 (4mm); gauge: 20–22 sts x 28–30 rows. Yarn C: Rowan Lurex Shimmer; color & code: Antique White Gold 332; needles: 3 (3.25mm); gauge: 29 sts x 41 rows.

PROJECT 21, BEADED POMPON HAT
Yarn: Jaeger Matchmaker Merino 4 ply; colors & codes: A = Cloud 744, B = Croquet 735; needles: 3 (3.25mm); gauge: 28 sts x 36 rows.

PROJECT 22, ZIGZAG PONCHO
Yarn: Rowan All Seasons Cotton; color & code: Cookie 169; needles: 7–9 (4.5–5.5mm); 16–18 sts x 23–25 rows.

PROJECT 23, CUTE CASUAL BAG
Yarn: Jaeger Extra Fine Merino Chunky; color & code: Hazel 016; needles: 10 (6mm); gauge: 15 sts x 20 rows.

PROJECT 24, STRIPED BEANIE
Yarn: Rowan Wool Cotton; colors & codes: A = Spark 947, B = Gypsy 910, C = Lavish 957; needles: 5–6 (3.75–4mm); gauge: 22–24 sts x 30–32 rows.

PROJECT 25, BEADED DENIM BAG
Yarn: Rowan Denim; color & code: Memphis 229; needles: 6 (4mm); gauge: 20 sts x 28 rows before washing, 20 sts x 32 rows after washing.

PROJECT 26, LACY BEADED HAT
Yarn: Rowan Wool Cotton; color & code: Hiss 952; needles: 5–6 (3.75–4mm); gauge: 22–24 sts x 30–32 rows.

PROJECT 27, FELTED BOOTIES
Yarn: Yorkshire Tweed DK; colors & codes: A = Sprinkle 353, B = Skip 347, C = Slosh 345; needles: 6 (4mm); gauge: 20–22 sts x 28–30 rows.

PROJECT 28, FLORAL RELIEF SCARF
Yarn: Rowan Wool Cotton; colors & codes: A = Gypsy 910, B = Lavish 957, C = Coffee Rich 956, D = Spark 947; needles: 5–6 (3.75–4mm); gauge: 22–24 sts x 30–32 rows.

PROJECT 29, SUMMER BAG AND COIN PURSE
Yarn: Rowan Cotton Glace; colors & codes: A = Pier 809, B = Sky 749, C = Zeal 813, D = Oyster 730, E = Shoot 814; needles: 3–5 (3.25–3.75mm); gauge: 23 sts x 32 rows.

PROJECT 30, DIMPLE STITCH SHAWL
Yarn: Jaeger Luxury Tweed; color & code: Kew Green 826; needles: 6 (4mm); gauge: 21–23 sts x 28–31 rows.

Suppliers
The yarns used in this book are available from good department stores and via mail-order and internet suppliers. You can also try the following:

ROWAN YARNS
US
Rowan USA
4 Townsend West, Suite 8
Nashua, New Hampshire 03064
Tel: (603) 886 5041 / 5043
Email: wfibers@aol.com

Canada
Diamond Yarn (Toronto)
155 Martin Ross, Unit 3
Toronto, Ontario M3J 2L9
Tel: (416) 736 6111
Email: diamond@diamondyarn.com
Website: www.diamondyarn.com

UK
Rowan Yarns
Green Lane Mill
Holmfirth, West Yorkshire HD9 2DX
Tel: 01484 681881
Website: www.knitrowan.com

Australia
Australian Country Spinners
314 Albert Street
Brunswick, Victoria 3056
Tel: (03) 9380 3888

New Zealand
Alterknitives
PO Box 47961
Tel: (64) 9 376 0337

JAEGER YARNS
Jaeger Handknits
Green Lane Mill
Holmfirth, West Yorkshire HD9 2DX
Tel: 01484 680050

PATONS & ANCHOR MAGIC YARNS
Coats Crafts UK
PO Box 22, Lingfield House
Lingfield Point, McMullen Road
Darlington DA1 1YQ
Consumer helpline: (+44) 1325 394 237
Email: consumer.ccuk@coats.com
Website: www.coatscrafts.co.uk

Index

Author's acknowledgments

Huge thanks to Kate Buller and Debbie Abrahams for making this possible, and to Ann Hinchliffe and everyone at Rowan Yarns/Jaeger Handknits for their help, support, and fantastic yarns. Thanks also to Kate Kirby and Michelle Pickering at Quarto for guiding me through this process; to Anthea McAlpin and Kathleen Dyne for help with knitting the projects; to Julie Marchington for knitting, listening, and generally being my sounding board; and to Mum (Marjorie Trotman) for teaching me to knit so long ago because I was bored! And finally to Sam Sloan, thanks for your patience … we can go out now.

All photographs and illustrations are the copyright of Quarto.